7

RITUALS
OF
SELF-MADE
MILLIONAIRES

Dr. Aleksander Šinigoj

7 Rituals of Self - Made Millionaires

Dr. Aleksander Šinigoj

ISBN-13: 978-1490531656

DISCLAIMER

This book is intended as an inspiration or motivation for anyone wishing to become a self-made millionaire in an honest, ethical way, but most importantly using a rational method and with a strictly calculated risk all the way through the process. Neither the author nor the publisher assume any responsibility for any errors or omissions, nor do they represent or warrant that the information, ideas, plans, actions, suggestions, and/or methods of operation contained herein are in all cases true, accurate, appropriate, or legal. It is the reader's responsibility to consult with his or her own advisor, or an expert for a specific area before putting any of the enclosed information, plans, examples, ideas, or practices into play. The author encourages the reader not to use any sort of leverage. The book includes a link to a free mind programming CD. The author and the publisher specifically disclaim any liability resulting from the application of the information contained in this book, and the information or any of the ideas are not intended to serve as legal advice related to individual situations.

All of the research, along with the entire book, is based on author's experiences and opinions. The author's model of the world, his values, beliefs and thinking processes represent limitations, which should be taken into account when reading the book. Further studying, skills and competencies and expert opinions should be taken into consideration before any action is taken.

We are what we repeatedly do. Excellence then, is not an act, but a habit.

ARISTOTLE

Contents

DEDICATION

I want to dedicate this book to my family. For their love and support.

And I want to also dedicate this book to one of you, one of my readers out there. Maybe you are the one who is reading this book right now. I am not sure if you have any formal education or not. I am not sure if you have any money or not. I am not sure if you think you deserve or do not deserve to become a millionaire. I am not sure whether you have a clear plan on how to do it, or you don't. I dedicate this book to YOU. I honestly think that no matter what your current position is, it can change; you can change it. If you will start changing your mind, your thoughts and your internal programs and rituals today, I believe miracles can happen tomorrow. Stay strong, stay positive. I know sometimes it might not be so simple. Smile, have fun and be persistent. I support you in your mission. I believe in you. I love you. Believe in the fact that after the rain and all the clouds are gone, the sky is really nice and clear. I believe there is a great power and potential inside of you. You have been given a gift of life and a purpose, which you can fully live when you tap into your potential. May this book help awaken some of that great potential inside of you.

THE JOURNEY

I have been studying successful people all over the world for the last few decades. Reading books, articles, watching biographies, meeting with successful and wealthy people face-to-face and conducting a series of interviews with them when they agreed. When it was not possible to meet, I settled for publicly available material. When I was interested in someone no longer living, I searched for books, articles, and material available on the Internet. Some of the people I studied were billionaires, some were multi-millionaires and some were simply rich or had achieved extraordinary results, which helped them to become rich. Please understand that to put all seven rituals into a format that is easy for me to express and is practical for you, my dear reader, I had to do some deleting, generalizing and distorting of information. In other words, I had to generalize and leave many details out, which I found to be a serious limitation of my book and the research on which my

THIS BOOK IS BEST USED SIMPLY AS A MODEL. YOU CAN FIND GUIDANCE AND YOUR OWN WAY TO IMPLEMENT THE MODEL AND TO USE THE SEVEN RITUALS THAT CAN HELP YOU BECOME A SELF-MADE MILLIONAIRE IN YOUR LIFE AND YOUR BUSINESS ENVIRONMENT.

book is based. However, that is why I also believe that this book is best used simply as a model. You can find guidance and your own way to implement the model and to use the

THE GOOD NEWS IS THAT THE OVERALL NUMBER OF SELF-MADE MILLIONAIRES AROUND THE WORLD IS GROWING.

seven rituals that can help you become a self-made million-aire in your life and your business environment.

According to *World Wealth Report*, in 2012, there were over 12 million people around the world that were millionaires, and the number is changing all the time from year to year and even during a specific year. Their definition of a millionaire is an individual with a net worth of at least one million dollars in all assets except their primary residence. Even though we might agree that there are some years when the number goes up and some years when the number goes down, the general trend and the good news is that the overall number of self-made millionaires around the world is growing. Due to new technologies and new ways of operating, but also due to markets that are easily accessible because of the Internet and all the improvements, there are more and more opportunities for you to become a millionaire. The speed that the world is changing is incredible and new success stories of people becoming self-made millionaires help us understand that it is time to be optimistic for the people who have the seven rituals in their life together with a strong wish to become self-made millionaires.

More really good news: you can be one of them in a much shorter time than in the past. There are new opportunities and more demand for new solutions to all sorts of problems that we did not even know we had. There is a need for products and services that can help people solve their problems and improve the quality of their lives. In this millennium it is far easier and far more quickly possible to become a self-made millionaire than at any time in

the past. At the same time, I urge you not to be impatient with your wealth and abundance, because impatience has often led to bad decisions, poverty and sleepless nights with many self-made millionaires. Also using leverage, borrowing other people's money, or any other financial activity that puts lots of risk and lots of pressure on the person or the company, many times does not help you to become a self-made millionaire. More about that topic in the following chapters.

There is one more thing I need to point out. After learning about the seven rituals and applying them to my life, my financial stability had an incredible shift. I started to build up financial habits and stability, which I had never before encountered before. This was also true in times of crises, at least what the media and the general public were calling crises. My business life and my income grew steadily and are still growing. At the time when I started to write this book I was not yet a self-made millionaire, perhaps the opposite. Still, I was shocked how well the principles and rituals that I explain

in this book work, by creating and bringing more money and more wealth into my life. And I was even more shocked at how those principles helped the lives of thousands of people

THE SEVENTH RITUAL IS THE RITUAL THAT MAKES THE DIFFERENCE FOR MOST PEOPLE

that I was teaching through numerous workshops all over the world. However, the more time passed, the more streams of income I managed to accumulate. I managed more wise and more sustainable investments and I was able to make smarter decisions. I got closer and closer to becoming a self-made millionaire. I am on my way there, and I invite you to join me.

Let me give you some more insights about the book that might be helpful to you before you dig in. You might have heard about the first six rituals before in different ways. Each of them is important and each of them differs from the context in which it is being presented. However, the seventh ritual is the ritual that makes the difference for most people and I believe that is the ritual, when mastered truly and profoundly, would help you create wealth, abundance and your first million or possibly your second, third, fourth, fifth, hundreds or even thousands of millions. The seventh ritual is about creating magic. What I mean by magic will be explained in the chapter on creating magic, but I believe that self-made millionaires are people who create magic in their professional or business lives. It is not the magic that you see on TV, but it is the seventh ritual,

IT IS THE SEVENTH RITUAL, WHICH I CALL THE MAGIC RITUAL, WHERE THE SELF-MADE MILLIONAIRES HAVE BEEN ABLE TO CONVERT THE IDEAS THAT THEY HAVE IN THEIR MINDS INTO PRODUCTS AND SERVICES, WHICH RESULT, AT THE END OF THE DAY, IN POSITIVE CASH FLOW.

which I call the magic ritual, where the self-made millionaires have been able to convert the ideas that they have in their minds into products and services, which result, at the end of the day, in positive cash flow and in becoming millionaires.

Please do not rush immediately to the chapter about the seventh ritual as many of the people did when they read the first edition of this book, but look at the initial six rituals first, because they are vital in creating or helping to create the ritual about creating magic. This journey can be easily done by yourself. At the same time, it will be more fun if you invite one more person to join you in this pursuit to become a self-made millionaire. This person can be your accountability partner. You can have several accountability partners. At the end of each ritual you have a special table where you can put their names. He or she might not only hold you accountable, but also support you and help you. You can do that formally, by hiring a coach, or informally, by inviting a friend that has similar dreams or wishes and together you can make a vow that you will both become self-made millionaires.

Before we go to the rituals and the rest of the book, let me express my deep, deep gratitude for your trust and belief when deciding to buy and read this book. We might have met personally, or not. I am not sure whether you have been to any of my workshops so far, or not. Perhaps after reading this book you would like to learn more and we may meet face to face at one of my workshops. In that case, I will repeat something about which I am absolutely sure: I do not know you and I do not know

> I BELIEVE YOU HAVE SO MUCH POTENTIAL INSIDE OF YOU THAT WHEN YOU UNLOCK ALL THAT POTENTIAL AND USE IT FULLY, THAT FULL POTENTIAL COMBINED WITH THE SEVEN RITUALS OF SELF-MADE MILLIONAIRES, MIRACLES CAN HAPPEN.

anything about you. But one thing I am absolutely sure about: You are born into this world and onto this planet to become rich and to live in abundance if you want it from your heart. If you desire and wish, I believe you can become a self-made millionaire. It is your birth right. I also believe you have so much potential inside of you that when you unlock all that potential and use it fully, that full potential combined with the seven rituals of self-made millionaires, miracles can happen. At that point, you can be on the path to your first million as well as to your financial freedom and financial abundance.

I am grateful for your investment in time and money to read this book. I pray that perhaps one sentence, one thought or one simple idea would improve your life and the lives of people around you. Use it to do more good on this planet.

To your millions,
Dr. Aleksander Šinigoj

It always seems impossible until it's done.

NELSON MANDELA

A RITUAL,
NOT A HABIT

Why did I choose the word ritual and not habit? The main reason and answer lie in language description: With a ritual we have more of a ceremony, more deliberation of action, but also respect for doing something special. Ritual means introducing a meaningful, worthy and really special habit into your life and your business life. And I want you to play with that concept of introducing something special, your millionaire rituals, into your life. You may call them habits if you like, but with my belief and my understanding of the word ritual, there is more to it; there is some secrecy, some magic, which led me to use this word. And I, of course, would like to encourage you to use the same word.

WITH A RITUAL WE HAVE MORE OF A CEREMONY, MORE DELIBERATION OF ACTION, BUT ALSO RESPECT FOR DOING SOMETHING SPECIAL.

When I started to study self-made millionaires, I found out, after my first year of studying, that it would be hard to find a recipe that would include all of the diversity and all the different stories involved in becoming a self-made millionaire. This would become a limitation in my research. Each self-made millionaire success story is different. And your story will be unique, too. If you decide to become a millionaire and implement the seven rituals, I am sure that your story will be different from any of

EACH SELF-MADE MILLIONAIRE SUCCESS STORY IS DIFFERENT.

the other stories. Even if you will model yourself after a particular self-made millionaire, you still need to consider your world according to particular market conditions, needs, the current world situation and challenges.

Go out yourself and study the rituals after you read the book; investigate self-made millionaires. You might discover similar answers and use similar ways of learning their recipe for success. The process is very simple if you want to get a feel for it, and more complex when you want to focus and look for details, trying to put all those variables into a model. In many cases it is both a time and money consuming process watching videos, traveling, and reading; but I loved it. There are so many ways you can approach this learning. You might observe and study about self-made millionaires by meeting with them face-to-face, working or studying with them or through videos, audio books or simply by reading about them through books, biographies, articles, etc. Reading a good book, listening to a good video or meeting with a person that inspires you, will change your thoughts, your feelings, sometimes even your values and your beliefs, and all those changes are the changes that can help you become a self-made millionaire faster.

READING A GOOD BOOK, LISTENING TO A GOOD VIDEO OR MEETING WITH A PERSON THAT INSPIRES YOU, WILL CHANGE YOUR THOUGHTS, YOUR FEELINGS, SOMETIMES EVEN YOUR VALUES AND YOUR BELIEFS.

Let's use a metaphor from cooking. When you think of a chef that is really good at preparing a meal, for example some pasta, there is probably a common procedure where he or she puts pasta in boiling water, adds some salt and when the pasta is done, takes it out and makes

EVEN STEVE JOBS HAD A SPECIAL "COOKING" PROCESS, WHICH WE COULD HAVE MODELED TO CREATE MAGNIFICENT PRODUCTS AND SERVICES.

some sauce and the pasta is ready to eat. We might change the procedure and still get good results, but if we first take the pasta and try to boil it without the water, the pasta will not cook and we would be unable to eat it. Or, we might be able to eat it, but we would get a completely different, unpleasant and non-chewable result. We could start cooking, at first using cookbooks, or asking other people how they do it. Usually when someone is preparing a meal, especially if cooking for the first time, he or she focuses on every single step quite consciously, measuring the exact ingredients. Therefore, the early rituals of a chef would be quite predictable, standardized and easy to copy or model, especially if we are using the same cookbook or recipe.

After mastering the rituals of preparing great foods, for example the ritual of preparing the pasta, then it will usually become a less standardized process, no cookbooks, but more of a natural process. We start cooking unconsciously, when there is also a place for some of the creativity, heart and passion. When all three kick in, the chef can make the foods really special. The foods that are then being created would become special and unique for that particular chef. And all rituals associated with that activity would often become unconscious. For example, when an expert chef adds salt according to his or her internal taste, we know that this ability to taste and add ingredients to make an excellent pasta has been developed through time. Pasta is, of course, a metaphor. Even Steve Jobs had a special "cooking" process, which we could have modeled to create magnificent products and services. His great "foods" were amazing products and services, which he created by using a special procedure and changed the world of music, phones, computing, etc.

IT IS THE SAME WHEN YOU TALK ABOUT RITUALS OF SELF-MADE MILLIONAIRES. THE RITUALS ARE DONE MANY TIMES, FIRST CONSCIOUSLY; AND THEN AFTER MANY, MANY YEARS THOSE RITUALS ARE DONE UNCONSCIOUSLY.

It is the same when you talk about rituals of self-made millionaires. The rituals are done many times, first consciously; and then after many, many years those rituals are done unconsciously, like breathing, without even paying too much attention to it. Remember that all those people have been in a similar situation to a chef consciously practicing his rituals until they became unconscious. People like Warren Buffett do not consciously think about the internal process of setting goals, dealing with challenges, being persistent and doing what is necessary to succeed. They do it in a way that seems natural to them, like breathing, but sometime in the past they consciously learned what they now do by trial and error, many times over.

THE MILLIONAIRE MENTAL ATTITUDE IS THE WINNING MENTAL ATTITUDE; ONE MUST BE WILLING TO PAY THE PRICE OF SUCCESS.

They developed a special mental attitude that allowed

them to persist and to work better and harder. The millionaire mental attitude is the winning mental attitude; one must be willing to pay the price of success. It is a mental atti-

MICHELANGELO WAS FORMING A VIRTUAL MASTERMIND ALLIANCE WITH GOD.

tude that can help you achieve what is necessary to achieve. And it is part of the rituals that I am going to write more about in the following chapters. I am quite confident that you could go out and repeat my study and do the same analysis and research, model successful people and find a self-made millionaire that does not have exactly those seven rituals, or even is violating one of them. Consider Michelangelo, one of the greatest artist of all times, who was perceived to be a self-made millionaire by the measures of that time. He studied and formed a mastermind alliance with many of his great teachers, but he also went away and did not use the mastermind ritual when he created his greatest works. He avoided crowds in order to spend time in solitude and to create some of the most wonderful artistic works of all times. He was forming a virtual mastermind alliance with God. In his own words, he stated that God was talking to him and helping him to create his masterpieces. You can do the same. There is more about creating virtual masterminds in the chapter dedicated to mastermind groups. And when you read more about virtual mastermind groups later on and you do not like it, then you do not need to implement it in your life. Pick only those rituals that you most need and want to have. It might be helpful for most people to have all of them, but you need to find your own way. Once you decide to become a self-made millionaire, I do not wish that you become obsessed with the

A RITUAL, NOT A HABIT 25

seven rituals, but simply use them as a special tool that can help you create your first, second and all the millions that will follow.

Please understand that the book has been written with my very best intentions, and the final research is simply my observation of the values, beliefs and strategies of self-made millionaires and how their worlds function. It is not a plan for you to implement after you finish reading it. My idea was to show you what I believe after years of studying self-made millionaires, to show what they have achieved and what their key rituals are. I have modeled their values, beliefs, and strategies by having my own observational limitations and my model of the world. If, in any part of the book, you discover and understand there is a great idea or a strategy that it is useful for yourself, take it for yourself and use it in your life. Take that strategy, study it, look at all the pros and cons, and only then implement it in your life.

Be rational in your thinking. I am a great believer of taking time to think. Take proper thinking time, like Michelangelo did to create his masterpieces. Take time to really think rationally. Switch all of the noises off, be by yourself and base your decisions on rational thinking with a visionary mind still in place. Before you make a key de-

DO NOT BECOME OBSESSED WITH THE SEVEN RITUALS, BUT SIMPLY USE THEM AS A SPECIAL TOOL THAT CAN HELP YOU CREATE YOUR FIRST, SECOND AND ALL THE MILLIONS THAT WILL FOLLOW.

IF, IN ANY PART OF THE BOOK, YOU DISCOVER AND UNDERSTAND THERE IS A GREAT IDEA OR A STRATEGY THAT IS USEFUL FOR YOURSELF, TAKE IT FOR YOURSELF AND USE IT IN YOUR LIFE.

cision write it down on a piece of paper, and then consider why you are going to make that key decision. The 'why' is crucial. And make sure that the 'why' is not only based on your financial goals. I will repeat that later in the book, but self-made millionaires, most of the time, did not have financial goals as primary goals. But the results of their success and their vision, the result of bringing massive value to customers and the market, were financial benefits that led them to become self-made millionaires. The more money they made, the better game

TAKE PROPER THINKING TIME, LIKE MICHELANGELO DID TO CREATE HIS MASTERPIECES. TAKE TIME TO REALLY THINK RATIONALLY.

CALCULATED RISK IS A PHRASE THAT REFERS TO AN ACTION THAT SELF-MADE MILLIONAIRES TAKE MANY TIMES, BUT REMEMBER TO FOCUS ON THE CALCULATED PART OF THE WORD.

they could play, so they used the money to be better at what they do.

Talk to experts in the field and then still calculate the risk. When you learn to work with risk in small decisions, you grow, and you learn how to mitigate risk with bigger decisions. Calculated risk is a phrase that refers to an action that self-made millionaires take many times, but remember to focus on the calculated part of the word. Many people that wanted to become millionaires overnight, with speculations, by using high risk moves or even making purchasing decisions without using their own money, have regretted those decisions; they are not the ones I have modeled here. They deserve a deep study and perhaps another book will be written about them. The self-made millionaires that I have modeled focused on improving the products and services all the time; their main goal was not money, but to live their passion and dreams. Most of the self-made millionaires that I have modeled have been millionaires for several years and I believe that, due to their discipline and focus, they will continue to be so in the future. But let's go into details later on in the book about some of the topics that I am discussing here.

IN THIS BOOK YOU CAN DISCOVER A STRUCTURED VIEW OF WHY SELF-MADE MILLIONAIRES ARE SO SUCCESSFUL AND HOW YOU CAN APPLY THE SAME PRINCIPLES AND RITUALS IN YOUR LIFE.

My theory in the book is based on what I discovered studying self-made millionaires and highly successful people, so in this book you can discover a structured view of *why* self-made millionaires are so successful and *how* you can apply the same principles and rituals in your life. I am discussing my view because I have not used any special statistical or quantitative method. My method is based on interviews and is qualitative. I am aware that I might have read many books, articles and video materials again and again, some of them more than a dozen times, and that I have my own values, beliefs and ways of perceiving and viewing reality, which could have led to my overrating some of the ideas and underrating or not seeing some other ideas. I suggest that when you read the book you use a pen to highlight the useful ideas, but also use a self-made millionaire implementation to-do list, which can be found at the end of each chapter. It will help you take action.

I am not sure what your main reason is for starting to read this book. Perhaps you would like to become a self-made millionaire, or you would simply like to have more financial stability and abundance in your life, or you are simply curious about what I might have to say. Whatever your reasons are for buying and reading this book, please look at how this research can help you.

THE QUESTIONS YOU SHOULD ASK YOURSELF: "HOW CAN I TAKE THE SEVEN RITUALS, LEARN THEM IN DETAILS AND IMPLEMENT THEM INTO MY LIFE IN THE WAY THAT WILL FIT MY NEEDS AND MY LIFE AND WHO I AM?"

There is a second part of this book, which starts with the questions you should ask yourself: "How can I take the seven rituals, learn them in details and implement them into my life in the way that will fit my needs and my life and who I am?" I am sure that you can beat the odds and enjoy your first millions without having all seven rituals. And the second part of your research, which I encourage you to do, is to look for those rituals in self-made millionaires you know and discover their rituals. I am also sure that you will find plenty of people who, when you first think of that person you would say, no way does that person have a ritual. There are some practical exercises at the end of each chapter and at the end of each ritual, which can help you and guide you on your way to becoming financially independent and wealthy.

Be yourself;
everyone else is
already taken.

OSCAR WILDE

FIND YOUR OWN MILLIONAIRE FORMULA

When you study self-made millionaires, or read this book, do not try to copy them literally. Be yourself. Do not pretend. Be who you truly are. I invite you to learn the rituals, but to use them according to your values and beliefs. I invite you to find and create your millionaire formula. Use your unique capabilities, your talents, be different than the rest of the world, but see how the rituals and the formula used by others can be used in your wealth creation. Do not automatically believe what I write and what I emphasize in my book; create your own opinion and your own process for critical thinking. Whatever I write is what I believed as important when I was studying self-made millionaires. I might have changed my mind by the time you are reading this book, although some of the rituals and principles I describe are timeless. Do not take that without critically studying it, consulting with experts or looking at what is first

> BE WHO YOU TRULY ARE.
> DO NOT AUTOMATICALLY
> BELIEVE WHAT I WRITE AND
> WHAT I EMPHASIZE IN MY
> BOOK; CREATE YOUR OWN
> OPINION AND YOUR OWN
> PROCESS FOR CRITICAL
> THINKING.

applicable to you and your business. And second, use what is really important to you and understand how you can use that knowledge and the rituals to your full advantage. Sometimes you might need to change your beliefs about who you are, about how to do business, about your capabilities, etc.

People who became self-made millionaires believed; they believed in what they were about to do, when no one else believed. And they remained true to themselves, to their ideals, vision, goals. And when you come to the seventh ritual, the magic ritual, you will see that powerful beliefs can help create results. Of course you always need to listen to the market, to the customers, see how you can solve problems, predict and exceed expectations, but also look at your balance sheet, be present and focused on what you do. You can not be a general if you lead your army from a safe hill miles from the battle. And remember that every battle is different from any other. Find strategies that fit your own personality and your own battles. When you look at self-made millionaires you will find strategies that are great, some that are fine and some that are useless to you. I am collecting strategies of self-made millionaires because I would like to learn not only about their rituals, but also how they implement those rituals. I am always questioning. What are the activities behind the core structure? When a strategy is applied individually, without considering other variables like beliefs and values of a particular person,

> **LISTEN TO THE MARKET, TO THE CUSTOMERS, SEE HOW YOU CAN SOLVE PROBLEMS, PREDICT AND EXCEED EXPECTATIONS, BUT ALSO LOOK AT YOUR BALANCE SHEET, BE PRESENT AND FOCUSED ON WHAT YOU DO.**

it might not be the best way to do it. Let me give you an example of a strategy that I like. It is from Warren Buffett, who encourages people not to use debt. There are several values and beliefs that Warren Buffett uses to support that specific strategy. He also directs people on focusing on what they do well with

DO NOT LOOK AT DISHONEST OR UNETHICAL PEOPLE AS YOUR ROLE MODELS AS YOU WILL HARDLY FIND THEM AMONG THE RICH PEOPLE OVER A LONGER PERIOD OF TIME.

passion and integrity. You can use that input to start creating your personal formula.

Coming from a background of Information Technology and from my second background of Neuro-linguistic programming, I understand and emphasize the importance of being precise and accurate with language, and that some mathematics and statistics can bring you closer to a millionaire model as well as a more precise formula than simple observations can. I also want to emphasize that studies and/or interviews of a small sample of a few hundred self-made millionaires that are generalized to millions of self-made millionaires might miss out on some information. I am repeating this, but it is important for you to truly look at my book from this perspective. The seven rituals of self-made millionaires is a millionaire formula based on facts; but it is also based on interpretations and information, distorted by what my observations were. My beliefs and my perceptions are with regard to the key seven rituals or ingredients, which made the self-made millionaires so successful. I am sure that if you go out and look at a specific self-made millionaire, he or she might have another extra ritual, or might not have one or two of the rituals that are mentioned here. You might find someone that has built his or her wealth unethically, or someone that won a lottery, or someone who made his or her millions without going the extra mile or working hard. My advice to you: Do not look at dishonest or unethical people as your role models as you will hardly find them among the rich people over a longer period of time.

Having said that, my main goal when studying the self made millionaire was to create a magic formula, a formula that would help recreate several new millionaires, people who would be able to learn and make more money easily and simply. My goal for the book is rather small, to create 10,000 new millionaires by 2024 anywhere around the world. First, I wanted a formula for myself, which would enable me to stop struggling and looking for money from month to month, or sometimes from week to week. That is why I started studying this topic. I was asking myself: "How is it possible that some people without any background or any formal education, facing all possible obstacles, without any money or connections, manage to push through and create immense abundance and become self-made millionaires? And how is it possible that some people, with all possible advantages in life, do little or are

"HOW IS IT POSSIBLE THAT SOME PEOPLE WITHOUT ANY BACKGROUND OR ANY FORMAL EDUCATION, FACING ALL POSSIBLE OBSTACLES, WITHOUT ANY MONEY OR CONNECTIONS, MANAGE TO PUSH THROUGH AND CREATE IMMENSE ABUNDANCE AND BECOME SELF-MADE MILLIONAIRES? AND HOW IS IT POSSIBLE THAT SOME PEOPLE, WITH ALL POSSIBLE ADVANTAGES IN LIFE, DO LITTLE OR ARE FAR FROM SELF-MADE MILLIONAIRES?"

far from self-made millionaires?" These questions opened new questions. I then started to look for the secret formula. Creating a formula based on human behavior is always a demanding task. My idea was to create a formula that the majority, if not all of the readers and people interested in becoming self-made millionaires, would be able to use.

I also wanted a formula for myself and then for all the participants of my workshops and all the readers of this book, which would enable all of us to understand a few basic principles and to use them to one's own advantage in order to become a self-made millionaire. I urge you to do that not only for yourself, but also to inspire others around you, all the people that you love and also the people that love you. Many other people that might see your example, how you became a self-made millionaire, would simply follow. Many times I am asked by parents how they can teach their kids the key basic principles that would enable them to have what they wanted in their lives, and I always give them the same answer: "When teaching kids, be what you want your kids to be. Do not teach them by words. Teach them by your example. And the more you change, the more they will be inspired to change." If you want your kids to be rich, you need to show them by example how you can do it, and let them do the same. They need to learn their way to make money and to be independent. Become a self-made millionaire so that your kids can learn by example and

> "WHEN TEACHING KIDS, BE WHAT YOU WANT YOUR KIDS TO BE. DO NOT TEACH THEM BY WORDS. TEACH THEM BY YOUR EXAMPLE. AND THE MORE YOU CHANGE, THE MORE THEY WILL BE INSPIRED TO CHANGE."

live in abundance when they grow.

The learning that I describe several times in my book is unconscious learning. We learn consciously, by observing or focusing our attention on what we are trying to learn. And we also learn unconsciously, without being aware of it, and one of the ways is by spending time with other people. After a while we may automatically, or unconsciously, repeat their language patterns, thinking patterns and behaviors without even being aware of doing it. That is why people say that a positive or negative mental attitude is contagious. Depression or anger or a negative mental attitude can be contagious. It is important that you spend as little time as possible with people who are negative or have negative mental attitudes. And if you have people like that in your family, or at your work place, use a simple trick to change their state of mind by diverting your conversation to topics that they are less negative about.

DEPRESSION OR ANGER OR A NEGATIVE MENTAL ATTITUDE CAN BE CONTAGIOUS. IT IS IMPORTANT THAT YOU SPEND AS LITTLE TIME AS POSSIBLE WITH PEOPLE WHO ARE NEGATIVE OR HAVE NEGATIVE MENTAL ATTITUDES.

THE SEVEN RITUALS OF SELF-MADE MILLIONAIRES ARE AN UNCONSCIOUS COMPETENCE OF SELF-MADE MILLIONAIRES.

Spend some time close to people that inspire you to learn both consciously and unconsciously. The challenge that I encountered when studying self-made millionaires, and you might be faced with the very same challenge, is that all of the seven rituals of self-made millionaires are an unconscious competence of self-made millionaires. They have been doing using these competencies for so long that they do not need to think consciously about it any longer. Most of them haven't learned the rituals consciously, but mastered them as a result of their persistence and determination to achieve what they wanted to achieve. It was a result of their secret formula, the ritual number 7. When you ask people who are good at what they do unconsciously, many times they have difficulties in teaching you their job because it includes so many different responses. It might include responses to their colleagues at work, to customers or suppliers, or when they need something urgently, when they fight for new ideas and changes within their businesses, etc. Therefore, modeling and looking for their formula is a complex process.

My goal for you is to start looking for your formula, for your winning recipe, which would enable you to become a self-made millionaire. When you find your right way to introduce the seven rituals for becoming a self-made millionaire and creating abundance, you will discover the real secret of the ritual number 7, which I have called the magic ritual. For now let's simply say this ritual is the one that really enables self-made millionaires to become and to remain wealthy, and it is the key ritual that really diversifies wealthy and rich people from others. And even though you might not see it clearly, or understand the details, after reading the book, make sure that you surround yourself with self-made millionaires that will consciously or unconsciously transfer the ritual

WHEN YOU FIND YOUR RIGHT WAY TO INTRODUCE THE SEVEN RITUALS FOR BECOMING A SELF-MADE MILLIONAIRE AND CREATING ABUNDANCE, YOU WILL DISCOVER THE REAL SECRET OF THE RITUAL NUMBER 7, WHICH I HAVE CALLED THE MAGIC RITUAL.

number 7 to you. You might use this ritual to your advantage to create and bring even more millions, and to create even more money in your life. I want to repeat this several times: With very few self-made millionaires the money was the end goal; it was merely a consequence or a result of their hard work and their ability to organize themselves and their businesses in such a way that it helped them produce great value for their customers and the market they were in, which in return produced their riches.

At the end of the book you will find a ritual formula that, if you apply it fully, it may help you become a self-made millionaire in months or years. Simply follow 'creating magic,' and apply the formula to your life. Start doing it today. The very moment you understand the formula, transfer it to your life by creating and executing your own plan. At the moment you close this book, you might feel inspired. This is the best moment to begin. Do no wait for the right moment, for the right conditions. It is never the right moment for people who do not become self-made millionaires. The right moment for you is now. Start learning, start focusing your attention, make small steps if that feels more comfortable, but keep on moving, have your end goal in your mind all the time. People who make a difference are people who go out in the world, start working on an idea and they learn and improve as they go along. Start doing it now, immediately. And remember to do it with wisdom. Many self-made millionaires told me that

THE RIGHT MOMENT FOR YOU IS NOW. START LEARNING, START FOCUSING YOUR ATTENTION, MAKE SMALL STEPS IF THAT FEELS MORE COMFORTABLE.

they would be far richer or that they could have spent less time becoming millionaires if it was not for some stupid mistakes. Maybe they weren't focused enough, or they put their money (or borrowed money) into projects that were not part of their core business.

Remember one of the best pieces of advice that Warren Buffet once gave: "You only have to do a very few things right in your life, so long as you don't do too many things wrong."

There are several self-made millionaires that I would like to thank for helping me write this book. Most of them you might never have heard of, or learned from. Some of them are mentioned, most of them aren't. You would not recognize many of them as millionaires if you met them. They do not drive fancy cars, nor do they have fancy clothes, yachts or several houses. But you can see a great passion and light in their eyes when they talk about what they do. Below I mention some of the best known and most famous, some of them billionaires and millionaires that I have studied through all possible media, articles, videos, biographies, books, interviews, observations, workshops, face-to-face, etc. They are:

Sir Richard Branson

Steve Jobs

REMEMBER ONE OF THE BEST PIECES OF ADVICE THAT WARREN BUFFET ONCE GAVE: "YOU ONLY HAVE TO DO A VERY FEW THINGS RIGHT IN YOUR LIFE, SO LONG AS YOU DON'T DO TOO MANY THINGS WRONG."

IT IS SO MUCH MORE FUN AND EASY TO LEARN WHEN YOU ENJOY IT.

Elon Musk
Napoleon Hill
Bill Gates
Keith Cunningham
Michelangelo
Michael Jordan
Warren Buffet
Anthony Robbins
Oprah Winfrey
Dr. Richard Bandler
Kathleen La Valle
John La Valle
Will Smith
Sir John Templeton
Sara Blakely
Brian Tracy
Charlie Munger
Victor Kiam
Andrew Carnegie
W. Clement Stone
J.K. Rowling
Henry Ford
and many others...

If I wanted to list all of them, this book would probably have too many pages. You can pick the same or similar ones that I have picked and study them. Look for ones that inspire you. Your list can be completely different than mine. Most importantly, make sure that when you study about self-made millionaires you enjoy learning about what they do. It is so much more fun and easy to learn when you enjoy it.

When it is obvious that the goals cannot be reached, don't adjust the goals, adjust the action steps.

CONFUCIUS

THE MATHEMATICS OF BECOMING A MILLIONAIRE

If you decide to become a self-made millionaire, you need to use a simple mathematical formula. Having a million dollars. Think about the formula that you are aiming at. It is very simple. Take away

THE RECIPE FOR LOSING WEIGHT FOR SOME PEOPLE IS EXTREMELY SIMPLE. THE ADVICE WOULD BE: "EAT LESS AND EXERCISE MORE." SIMPLE ISN'T IT?

your apartment or your house, where you live at the moment. The net value of your home is not included in the formula. When you take that away, your goal is to have a net value of all your assets exceed one million dollars or a similar amount in Euros, British Pounds or other currency. That's all. Simple, isn't it? There are many ways to achieve that. Sometimes I like to joke about the recipe for losing weight for some people is extremely simple. If I write a book about it, the advice would be: "Eat less and exercise more." Simple isn't it? Of course, it is more than that, but if you follow that simple piece of advice in a healthy manner, consulting with a dietitian or a medical doctor, you can quickly get to your ideal body weight with strong discipline, and, perhaps, with the help of a mentor.

The mentor can serve as a motivator or coach, or as your mastermind group member. And the idea of an ideal body weight it is quite simple, isn't it? I am sure that you believe that it is achievable to you if you are not there yet. It is achievable to anyone if they follow this simple formula or procedure with discipline. So eat less, eat healthily and exercise more. If you check your health with a specialist and simply step on the digital scale at home every morning, you would know how well you are doing and in which direction you are going.

Let's apply the same formula for becoming a millionaire. The idea is very simple and very basic. Earn more and spend less is a simple millionaire's formula. Both parts of the equation can help you get to your first million. After people start earning more, sometimes they start spending more. Not the best and quickest way to become a self-made millionaire. This is especially true if spending is outside of your business growth. It is like speeding up your car, and at the same time pressing harder on the brake. The more you speed up, the harder you press on the brake. Not good for the car and not a great driving experience, is it? Many of the self-made millionaires that I have studied reinvest money in their business or reinvest profits in growing their companies, but are very careful and observant in their spending on any luxuries at first. In my

EARN MORE AND SPEND LESS IS A SIMPLE MILLIONAIRE'S FORMULA. BOTH PARTS OF THE EQUATION CAN HELP YOU GET TO YOUR FIRST MILLION. AFTER PEOPLE START EARNING MORE, SOMETIMES THEY START SPENDING MORE. NOT THE BEST AND QUICKEST WAY TO BECOME A SELF-MADE MILLIONAIRE.

studies I have found many million-aires who do not own second homes, some of them drive seven or eight year old cars, some always buy second hand cars, do their shopping for clothes at big sales events and carefully plan their spending budget and are quite disciplined about that. Remember that the seven rituals that will be introduced to you in the next chapter have a great power to bring more wealth and more money into your life. The question that remains, of course, is how are you going to be disciplined with that money, which can help you materialize your thoughts? Spending it immediately as you make it will not allow you to make it as quickly to a million. On the other hand, strict discipline and being really careful might, for some people, be too hard or would mean that they would have to give up on some of their passions, like cars, traveling, clothes, houses, etc. Find your own balance.

Remember that losing weight mathematically is quite simple. And making your first million is also simple when you do the actual math. If you have the discipline and you follow the mathematical formula described above, it could be only a matter of time and per-

SPENDING IT IMMEDIATELY AS YOU MAKE IT WILL NOT ALLOW YOU TO MAKE IT AS QUICKLY TO A MILLION. FIND YOUR OWN BALANCE.

IF YOU HAVE THE DISCIPLINE AND YOU FOLLOW THE MATHEMATICAL FORMULA DESCRIBED ABOVE, IT COULD BE ONLY A MATTER OF TIME AND PERSISTENCE UNTIL YOU BECOME A SELF-MADE MILLIONAIRE. THE MILLION IN THE EQUATION IS HELD CONSTANT; YOU NOW NEED TO CHANGE AND INCREASE YOUR REVENUE. AND YOU NEED TO DECREASE YOUR EXPENDITURES OR COSTS.

sistence until you become a self-made millionaire. The million in the equation is held constant; you now need to change and increase your revenue. And you need to decrease your expenditures or costs. In theory, if tomorrow you make a sale where you make one million dollars after taxes, you are already there. But if you go more slowly, if you make more than you spend every month and you are disciplined, each month you are one step closer to your first million. And remember that the bigger the gap between your income and your costs or spending, the bigger steps you are making towards your million. So keep the mathematical formula in mind. Too many times people forget the strong discipline that self-made millionaires have on their spending, not only on making more money and increasing their revenues. So remember to do that, too, and I am sure you will be on your way to your first million more quickly. Think of all the items that you can eliminate from your budget and all the ways in which you can influence your income in a positive way. And still have fun. If you decide on something you really want to buy for yourself as a reward for doing well so many weeks or months, do it, but then go back to your discipline as quickly as possible. Go back to the seven rituals and the right mental attitude that I am going to describe to you in the next chapters. These will help you in both parts of this simple mathematical equation.

Figure 1: SELF-MADE MILLIONAIRE FORMULA

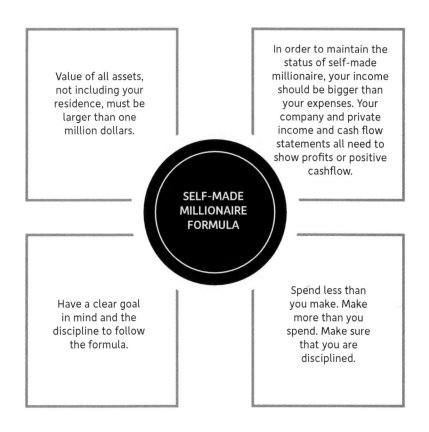

Value of all assets, not including your residence, must be larger than one million dollars.

In order to maintain the status of self-made millionaire, your income should be bigger than your expenses. Your company and private income and cash flow statements all need to show profits or positive cashflow.

SELF-MADE MILLIONAIRE FORMULA

Have a clear goal in mind and the discipline to follow the formula.

Spend less than you make. Make more than you spend. Make sure that you are disciplined.

The positive mental attitude is the right mental attitude... comprised of the 'plus' characteristics symbolized by such words as faith, integrity, hope, optimism, courage, initiative, generosity, tolerance, tact, kindliness and good common sense.

W. CLEMENT STONE

MILLIONAIRE MENTAL ATTITUDE

A ritual that I am going to depict before I describe the seven rituals is one that you can easily observe in people that are self-made millionaires, but it is the ritual that allows for the rest of the rituals and especially for the ritual number 7, the 'creating magic' ritual, to come true. A millionaire mental attitude is a way of thinking, or a ritual, that can be learned by practicing thinking like a millionaire, acting like one and feeling like a self-made millionaire, first consciously; then, after a while, it becomes automatic or unconscious. In his book, Think and Grow Rich, Napoleon Hill speaks about positive mental attitude. Also, along with his student and later associate, W. Clement Stone, Hill has written an excellent book, Success Through a Positive Mental Attitude, which I would recommend, especially if you work in sales, direct sales, multilevel marketing or the insurance business. I would encourage you to study both books in

> A MILLIONAIRE MENTAL ATTITUDE IS A WAY OF THINKING, OR A RITUAL, THAT CAN BE LEARNED BY PRACTICING THINKING LIKE A MILLIONAIRE, ACTING LIKE ONE AND FEELING LIKE A SELF-MADE MILLIONAIRE, FIRST CONSCIOUSLY; THEN, AFTER A WHILE, IT BECOMES AUTOMATIC OR UNCONSCIOUS.

great detail. They might also be a great gift for the people that you love if you want to give them something special. Both books are classics in the field of mind control and wealth creation.

A millionaire mental attitude is a similar attitude to that described by Hill and Stone, where we have a ritual of thinking of goals and solutions that create wealth and abundance. It is a problem solving attitude, and an attitude where, if an entrepreneur encounters an obstacle, he or she goes out and does everything necessary to make the goal come true and to make the solution work. The millionaire mental attitude really means that, in order to become a millionaire, I am willing to pay the price, to do whatever it takes to make it happen.

A MILLIONAIRE MENTAL ATTITUDE MEANS THAT YOU COULD BE FACED WITH SITUATIONS AND DIFFICULTIES WHERE YOU MIGHT NOT FIND A WAY OUT, NOT IMMEDIATELY AT LEAST, AND IT WOULD REQUIRE LOADS OF FAITH AND PERSISTENCE. BUT YOU WOULD PUSH THROUGH – YOUR THOUGHTS, YOUR FEELINGS AND YOUR ACTIONS WOULD RADIATE HOPE AND POSITIVE EXPECTATIONS.

It is an attitude where a self-made millionaire might not be smiling at the challenges that come towards them, but for sure he or she would push hard and would do whatever is necessary to make the plan or the idea a reality. The millionaire mental attitude is possible to learn. And you can learn it by changing your internal programs and your internal mind map in order to have, day by day, a positive mental attitude.

For some self-made millionaires, the millionaire mental attitude means that sometimes you are must work long hours or you are willing to study hard and improve in your field. A millionaire mental attitude means that you could be faced with situations and difficulties where you might not find a way out, not immediately at least, and it would require loads of faith and persistence. But you would push through – your thoughts, your feelings and your actions would radiate hope and positive expectations. Expectancy of creating great value products and services that would bring you millions. Believing that if you were given a problem, that there is a solution within you

A SELF-MADE MILLIONAIRE WITH A MILLIONAIRE MENTAL ATTITUDE PERSISTS, CONTINUES, FINDS A SOLUTION WHEN AND WHERE EVERYONE ELSE WOULD THINK IT IS NOT POSSIBLE; A SELF-MADE MILLIONAIRE CREATES A SOLUTION OR CREATES THE NECESSARY CONDITIONS FOR THE SOLUTION TO COME TRUE AND HAPPEN.

and you just need to uncover it, sleep on it; be creative. Looking for what you might not see. Anyone else might have quit, but a self-made millionaire with a millionaire mental attitude persists, continues, finds a solution when and where everyone else would think it is not possible; a self-made millionaire creates a solution or creates the necessary conditions for the solution to come true and happen. The millionaire mental attitude is paying the price, is doing whatever is necessary in order to make things happen and come true. A millionaire mental attitude is like a switch within you. Wouldn't now be a good time to switch that mental attitude on?

You can start working on the ritual yourself, first by thinking of yourself as a millionaire and acting as a millionaire. This is definitely a ritual that can help you achieve and help you have all the other rituals easily come true. The million-aire mental attitude is a ritual that requires you to see and look for opportunities, to look for good in adversities and to challenge any beliefs or any circumstances. When a problem or an obstacle comes, it means looking for a solution, looking for a solution that is not yet there. Remember that thoughts influence your feelings. Your feelings have a great influence on your behavior. Your behavior and your actions will lead to your results. So if your desired result will be to become a millionaire, you need to start with your thoughts and with your mental attitude.

> YOUR BEHAVIOR AND YOUR ACTIONS WILL LEAD TO YOUR RESULTS. SO IF YOUR DESIRED RESULT WILL BE TO BECOME A MILLIONAIRE, YOU NEED TO START WITH YOUR THOUGHTS AND WITH YOUR MENTAL ATTITUDE.

tal attitude. Think thoughts of inspiration, success, freedom, happiness and gratitude. Focus your thoughts on how to serve people and how to truly and honestly make a difference. The difference in your mental attitude can bring you to the first step on your road to becoming a self-made millionaire.

Figure 2: MILLIONAIRE MENTAL ATTITUDE

Speak, think and feel like you are already a millionaire. Focus your thoughts in the direction you want to go.

Your mental attitude, your thoughts, everything you do should be filled with faith, positive beliefs, positive words and you should always be thinking about new possibilities.

MILLIONAIRE MENTAL ATTITUDE

When you find an obstacle, simply believe that for every problem there is a solution.

Eat healthily, exercise, drink plenty of water, and sleep well. Do all the necessary things for you to be healthy in order to have passion and to maintain the ability to take action towards your goals.

I've come to believe that each of us has a personal calling that's as unique as a fingerprint - and that the best way to succeed is to discover what you love and then find a way to offer it to others in the form of service, working hard, and also allowing the energy of the universe to lead you.

OPRAH WINFREY

RITUAL 1: DIRECTION

Self-made millionaires know where they want to go. Their direction is clear. Direction regarding where one wants to go in his or her business-life and career is one of the starting rituals for success. From my study, I discovered that the self-made millionaires know what they want. They often look in the direction where they want to go. They think about it, dream about it and some are even obsessed with it. They are so clear about what they want when they talk, and you can see it in how they talk, how they move, how they act. Some of them knew what they wanted in their life; they knew their direction, their calling, from the beginning, from their youth. Some of them found their passion "accidentally" by trial and error, or by simply trying out different things or having a hobby and discovering what they really love doing and directed their lives and businesses in that direction. Self-made millionaires have a ritual of knowing

> DIRECTION REGARDING WHERE ONE WANTS TO GO IN HIS OR HER BUSINESS-LIFE AND CAREER IS ONE OF THE STARTING RITUALS FOR SUCCESS.

> SELF-MADE MILLIONAIRES HAVE A RITUAL OF KNOWING AND THINKING ABOUT THE DIRECTION THEY ARE GOING EVERY SINGLE DAY.

and thinking about the direction they are going every single day. Remember that the direction for most of them was not linear, and there were many obstacles on that path, but self-made millionaires found their way back to the direction in which they would like to go. The ritual of constantly thinking of what you want, and about the direction you want to go, is essential because you can program your unconscious mind to help you move towards that direction faster.

Self-made millionaires sometimes started by doing something they love. It was like a hobby for them at first, and had some short term goals. But when the hobby grew and become a serious business, their goals began changing and expanding, and their ritual about direction became simply a way of thinking and living. The direction ritual is not only about a direction, but also about thinking of constantly improving and improving to become better and better, to provide better products or services for clients, thinking about doing better than before; which we refer to as the 'extra mile' ritual later on. Again, many self-made millionaires knew from the beginning, and had a big compelling vision of who they wanted to become, or how they wanted to impact the world. But at the same time, they did not know how to do it or did not clearly see the end result. The ritual of thinking and knowing where you want to go does not

THE DIRECTION RITUAL IS NOT ONLY ABOUT A DIRECTION, BUT ALSO ABOUT THINKING OF CONSTANTLY IMPROVING AND IMPROVING TO BECOME BETTER AND BETTER, TO PROVIDE BETTER PRODUCTS OR SERVICES FOR CLIENTS, THINKING ABOUT DOING BETTER THAN BEFORE; WHICH WE REFER TO AS THE 'EXTRA MILE' RITUAL LATER ON.

need to include every single detail or a clear direction right until the end. Some self-made millionaires did not know exactly how they were going to get there; they kept changing and refining the goals and plans according to market response, customer response, and from the opportunities that had arisen.

IF YOU DO NOT KNOW WHERE YOU WANT TO GO WITH YOUR CAR – EVEN THE BEST CAR WITH THE BEST GPS OR BEST NAVIGATION SYSTEM CANNOT HELP YOU.

Imagine something like a GPS, or any other kind of satellite navigation system that you can have in your car or on your mobile phone. If you enter an exact town, street and street number, the GPS is going to take you where you want to go. If you get lost or get off the track, the system needs to recalculate and prepare a new route for you. The goal or target remains the same, but because the outer conditions changed, the plan changed; and if you follow the new directions and the new plan that the GPS prepares for you, you will take a different route, but ultimately reach the goal. That is the flexibility that we have when traveling, as many roads lead to Rome. The more we get lost or go off the track when we travel, the bigger the changes will be for the newly calculated GPS plan. It will provide us with a different route, with more adjustments, which we need in order to reach our destination.

Using the same metaphor of GPS, imagine this: If you do not know where you want to go with your car – even the best car with the best GPS or best navigation system cannot help you. In the same way you, no matter how much potential you have within you, no matter what you know or could do with all that knowledge, you cannot use that potential if you do not have a clear direction of where to go. If you still haven't decided where you want to use your potential, you have the same problem. Clarity brings power to your decisions and also gives you your inner strength. Many times it helps to have faith in order to continue to move towards your desired direction. Remember that you do not need to have a clear picture for all the necessary steps ten years in advance. Also, you do not need to have a clear plan, even GPS adjusts the plan according to the new route calculation when you go off track. You may have a clear vision about where you want to go ultimately, but you can leave that vision in the background and not be too specific. That vision, or that knowing clearly in which direction you want to go, can help you understand whether you are or are not going in the right direction.

If you sell warm winter clothes in hot summer, this might not be what the market really needs or wants. If Henry Ford had sold mobile applications in his time, it would not have been a good idea as no one had a mobile phone back then. If you would start producing a Ford Model T today, with the same characteristics as back then, it might not be the right time to do it. Doing the right thing at the right moment is going in the right direction. Doing wrong things, things that the market does not need or want is going in the wrong direction. To discover the right direction, you need not only listen to the market but also create a vision that could help to improve the quality of people's lives and solve their problems. You are in the business because you have customers. Move in the direction where you will have customers.

Sometimes people get lost, bored or stuck when traveling and would like to quit or go in another direction. It is the same with wish-to-be overnight self-made millionaires, who tend to quit very quickly. Remember that winners never quit and quitters never win. People more easily quit when they do something for the wrong reason. And money is not really a great motivator, at least not in the long run. One of the myths that people have about self-made millionaires is that they do what they do for the sake of money. Many of the people I met personally, and the people that I have studied during my research, have so much money that they do not need to work anymore. Not even their children, grandchildren and great grandchildren would have to work. And they still think, talk and move in the direction of their new goals. All the time. Remember when the majority of self-made millionaires started from zero or little money, many of them came out of poverty, but their goals were more about how they could serve the people, how they could make a difference and change or improve people's lives, or how they could improve their product or service. Money is important, but you can learn from different experiences by using it.

For knowing your direction, you need to know where you are right now. And to be honest about it. If the GPS system is not clear about your current position, any plan, any advice on direction, or a map given would be worthless. And you might not be in a position where you are proud or happy to be. I

WINNERS NEVER QUIT AND QUITTERS NEVER WIN.

REMEMBER: NO MATTER HOW LOST YOU GET USING A GPS, THERE IS ALWAYS A PLAN, THERE IS ALWAYS A SOLUTION FOR GETTING FROM POINT A TO POINT B. POINT A IS WHERE YOU ARE NOW AND POINT B IS THE DIRECTION WHERE YOU WANT TO BE AS A SELF-MADE MILLIONAIRE.

was deeply in debt and hopeless before I started studying and discovered the formula I am now helping others and myself with. Remember: No matter how lost you get using a GPS, there is always a plan, there is always a solution for getting from point A to point B. Point A is where you are now and point B is the direction where you want to be as a self-made millionaire. Ritual number one can help you get there. Once you know where you want to go, it is easier for other rituals to support you and help you get there. You might have some savings, or not. You might have some money, or not. You might be in a position where you still do not see the light in front of you, but you can change your life by changing your rituals, which can change your thinking process. Think more about what you want and where you want to go.

The law of cause and effect is part of how we think about this world. People who strive to become self-made millionaires only focus on the effect, on the end result, the money, but forget the cause. Focus more, with your mind and thoughts on the cause. When you think about how our world is organized, we have cause and effect in most of our thinking and living. When you work in a garden, plant and look after your flowers and water them carefully. That is the cause. The effect is that when you go out after a while and visit your garden, you expect to have nice flowers. The better the job you have done as a gardener, the more effort, studying, learning, improving, taking care of, the more likely

> THE LAW OF CAUSE AND EFFECT IS PART OF HOW WE THINK ABOUT THIS WORLD. PEOPLE WHO STRIVE TO BECOME SELF-MADE MILLIONAIRES ONLY FOCUS ON THE EFFECT, ON THE END RESULT, THE MONEY, BUT FORGET THE CAUSE.

you are to expect nice, wonderful flowers. So the flowers are the effect side of the equation. You never expect nice flowers if you or someone else did not plant them, or you plant them but did not take care of them. Self-made millionaires look at the cause part of the equation and the effect. The consequence of their focus is, of course, the money, their millions. The money comes naturally and automatically as an effect when you take care of the cause part of the equation. The direction ritual is about focusing on the actual cause, that is, on products and services. Focusing on adding value to the customer. Remember that they need the money to put back into more cause, into their products and services, because that is what they love doing anyway. So the cause and effect formula and the ritual of direction are both very clear to self-made millionaires. And they have a ritual of thinking about in which direction they can go to create the best possible cause. Many times when you look at people who struggle with money you will notice that they are focusing on the other part of the equation, they focus on the flowers part; they only wish for the money, but they do not think about the process that creates the wonderful flowers. Instead of loving all the small steps that bring out flowers, they simply love the flowers or the resulting money (the effect), but forget the steps (the cause) that led to the flowers. Some people even hate those steps

THE MONEY COMES NATURALLY AND AUTOMATICALLY AS AN EFFECT WHEN YOU TAKE CARE OF THE CAUSE PART OF THE EQUATION. THE DIRECTION RITUAL IS ABOUT FOCUSING ON THE ACTUAL CAUSE, THAT IS, ON PRODUCTS AND SERVICES. FOCUSING ON ADDING VALUE TO THE CUSTOMER.

and need coaching, mentoring, motivation, hypnosis, changing of their beliefs, value systems, etc., to make those necessary steps. For me as a trainer and a coach, it is great news, as I have full classrooms and I am booked sometimes months in advance. But when you think about it, it is truly simple. Focus on the cause, the effect will follow. Do the cause with passion, plant the flowers with love and passion, take care of them and your garden will look magnificent.

It is the same way with money. People who are broke want more money. They focus on how they can make more money. But they look at the effect and not at the cause. I want X amount of money or I want to be a millionaire is the side effect side. They go out and look for ways to create money. The self-made millionaires, at least the ones I studied, first found out what they wanted and had a direction or a vision of where they wanted to go and what they wanted to do. The money was a result of that vision. First they thought about a service or a product they want to give to others. Then they worked with great passion on that idea, and only then did they go out and earn the money, which was the consequence of their hard work and effort. The end result was their wealth. Many of the self-made millionaires reinvested the money back into their business, which helped their business to grow. I am not saying money is not important. The end goal, or the vision of self-made millionaires, was and still is to provide ultimate products and services, make great deals or improve customer satisfaction or customer experience.

If you find a million dollars to be too big of a goal, start with a hundred thousand first, or even ten thousand, put a deadline to it. Make sure you clearly define what kind of customer experience you want to offer and what type of effort you are going to put into the project in order to be able to achieve that goal. What will be the cause that will enable you to reach the desired effect? During my work as a trainer and a coach, I have had lots of clients who do not know clearly what their direction is or where they would like to go in life. If you want to start with the

THE END GOAL, OR THE VISION OF SELF-MADE MILLIONAIRES, WAS AND STILL IS TO PROVIDE ULTIMATE PRODUCTS AND SERVICES, MAKE GREAT DEALS OR IMPROVE CUSTOMER SATISFACTION OR CUSTOMER EXPERIENCE.

first ritual and do not know where to go, then simply think of not knowing where you want to go as an opportunity to find that out. When people tell me this with that sad and unsure face, I smile and say "That is great – if you do not know where you want to go, set a goal to find out what you want to do with your life." In that case, your first step should be setting a direction to discover where you want to go or to discover which direction is best for you. The next step that needs to done by anyone that is not clear about their purpose, their mission in life, or what they want to do, is to direct his or her mind to first clarify their life direction. There are limitless opportunities in this world at this very moment. You simply set up a goal to have a goal. Discover first what you would like to do in life and how can you help the world to be better with your unique talents and your contributions. Remember that most self-made millionaires did not know exactly what they wanted to do, but through inspired action, by making many mistakes or testing out different things, in the end they discovered their passion or they found a niche passion within their passion. And since that time, their ritual has always looked in the direction where they wanted to go. Looking, thinking, speaking about your desired goal is like programing the GPS. The major difference, however, is that the GPS might require that you program it once, but your mind requires lots of repetition and focused attention – it requires a ritual.

LOOKING, THINKING, SPEAKING ABOUT YOUR DESIRED GOAL IS LIKE PROGRAMING THE GPS. THE MAJOR DIFFERENCE, HOWEVER, IS THAT THE GPS MIGHT REQUIRE THAT YOU PROGRAM IT ONCE, BUT YOUR MIND REQUIRES LOTS OF REPETITION AND FOCUSED ATTENTION – IT REQUIRES A RITUAL.

Read your goals aloud, write them down; read them over with great passion every single day. Some athletes have said to me that their desire for a medal was in their mind, in their words, so often every single day. After awhile they felt it in their bodies; they felt it in every cell. When this happens, then you are on autopilot to get where you want to go. At that moment the unconscious mind, your internal GPS, will bring you anywhere you want to go. Make sure that by thinking, feeling and speaking about your goal, about your direction, this ritual comes from your brain and mind, to every cell of your body. It might take a day, a month, a year, or even longer. But keep focusing and keep thinking in that direction. It should be deeply integrated and a part of your autopilot, your unconscious mind. Ritual number one is so vital, that if you only implement this one, it will automatically bring other rituals into your life faster. Think about what you want in your life. Think about direction. Become so obsessed that you remove all negative thoughts. Make it a ritual to think about where you are going.

Figure 3: DIRECTION RITUAL

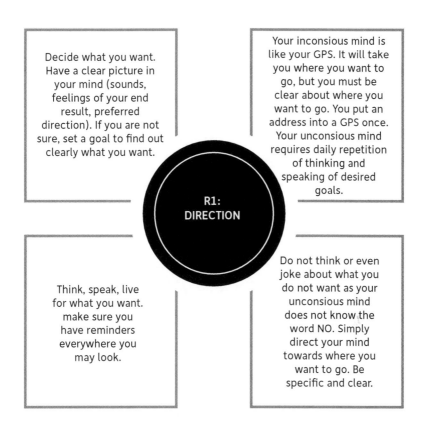

Decide what you want. Have a clear picture in your mind (sounds, feelings of your end result, preferred direction). If you are not sure, set a goal to find out clearly what you want.

Your inconsious mind is like your GPS. It will take you where you want to go, but you must be clear about where you want to go. You put an address into a GPS once. Your unconsious mind requires daily repetition of thinking and speaking of desired goals.

R1: DIRECTION

Think, speak, live for what you want. make sure you have reminders everywhere you may look.

Do not think or even joke about what you do not want as your unconscious mind does not know the word NO. Simply direct your mind towards where you want to go. Be specific and clear.

SELF ASSESSMENT QUESTIONS – YOUR MILLIONAIRE METER FOR RITUAL NUMBER 1, DIRECTION AND KNOWING WHAT YOU WANT:

• How well do you know what you want?

• How much precision will be in your actions?

• How well and clearly can you define your goals?

• Do you have a specific plan for achieving your goals?

• What is your mission in life?

• What is your vision?

• What are you good at?

• What would you do if you had all the money that you need for your life?

• What would you do if you knew you could not fail?

• Do you love what you do?

• Do you do what you love?

• What could you do that would bring out the best of your potential?

• Do you write down and read aloud your goals each and every day to program your unconscious mind on where to go?

TIPS THAT CAN HELP YOU BECOME A MILLIONAIRE BY YOUR KNOWING WHAT YOU WANT - DIRECTION:

- Be clear on what your ultimate goal or vision is!
- Visualize your target by pictures, sounds and feelings to program your mind on where to go.
- Visualize not only the end result, but also the desired behavior that you would like to exhibit.
- You can do it, believe. Believe in yourself and believe in your goal.
- Focus, focus and focus. Focus on what you do well.
- Keep changing your plan like a GPS, and always remember to look at where you are going.
- Remember, the secret is not only doing things that will help you become a self-made millionaire, but also not doing things that will not make you a self-made millionaire. Direction really means both -- where you are going and where you are not going.

SELF-MADE MILLIONAIRE IMPLEMENTATION LIST TO DO

After you read this chapter, think of how you can make your ideas become a reality. What will you do, and when and how you will do it? How will you think more about where you are going and less about where you don't want to go? How will you become clearer about the direction of where you want to go? Make sure you calculate any risks you might want to take, and study or communicate your decisions with people that can help you with that and are experts in the field. Also, think of who can be your accountability partner or your millionaire mastermind partner or partners? You can have multiple accountability partners depending on the activity. Or you might have none if you are really self-disciplined and you will easily do simple tasks on your own.

SELF-MADE MILLIONAIRE IMPLEMENTATION LIST TO DO

What are you going to do?	By when?	Your accountability partner

Vision without execution is just hallucination.

HENRY FORD

RITUAL 2:
HEARTY, PASSIONATE ACTION

SELF-MADE MILLIONAIRES KNOW WHAT THEY WANT AND WORK TOWARD GETTING IT DAY BY DAY. AND THEY ARE FASTER TO ACHIEVE IT WITH PASSION AND WITH DETERMINED ACTION.

We discovered the first ritual, which states that self-made millionaires know what they want and work toward getting it day by day. And they are faster to achieve it with passion and with determined action. So, the second ritual is 'taking action with a hearty passion.' Many people have wishes, but they only remain wishes. The desire and passion that self-made millionaires put into what they do is an extremely important ritual that helps them to move towards their results and pass all the obstacles they encounter. They have an enormous passion for what they do and a strong desire and powerful determination. They believe they can do it, and they believe that it is possible to do it. Sometimes the passion comes out of a passion or stubbornness for solving problems. They need to solve a problem and sometimes cannot sleep, nor do anything else, until they either find a solution or realize that the problem cannot be solved.

Think of something simple, like planting a flower in your garden. If you wanted the consequence, a wonderful shining flower in your garden, you first need ritual number 1: A desired outcome or goal. Once you set that goal, you need to take action, plant the flower. If you only visualize and think about it, it is not enough. Do not think only about the cause that we talked about in the previous chapter, but also act upon. It is vital. If you take action and you do it with passion,

WHEN YOU THINK OF PEOPLE WHO ARE SELF-MADE MILLIONAIRES, YOU CAN EASILY UNDERSTAND THAT THEY ARE SELF-MADE MILLIONAIRES SIMPLY BECAUSE THEY PROVIDED A GREAT PRODUCT OR SERVICE THAT WAS BASED ON THE PRINCIPLE OF TAKING ACTION WITH ALL THAT HEARTY ENERGY.

love and care, you might read more about how to protect that plant, carefully water it, etc. And after so many trials and errors, learning, after taking action that is needed, your flower will grow and shine. In the future, you might become a leading world authority on how to plant flowers. Follow the same path when you want to create your first million. When you think of people who are self-made millionaires, you can easily understand that they are self-made millionaires simply because they provided a great product or service that was based on the principle of taking action with all that hearty energy. Did you know that the heart has far more energy than the brain? Money came as a consequence or as a result of taking action, massive action with a hearty passion.

If you have an idea, an idea that you would like to implement and you keep thinking about that idea, and preparing a plan in your mind about that idea, your mind is working on ritual number 1, the direction ritual. At the same time, there is a possibility that the same idea, someplace else in this country or some other country, is being considered by ten, twenty or more people. It has been my experience, that many times I had an idea, I kept thinking about it, but I did not take any action. And later on, sometime after that, I saw or found somebody else actually taking action to implement "my" idea. Or I kept thinking about that idea, sometimes for years, and when I finally did it, I wished I had done it years ago. It would have made me rich. I do not like the belief that the idea is one percent of a successful project, while the other 99 percent is the execution. I believe that many times having the right direction and idea can save the action from going in the wrong direction. But truthfully, at the same time, an idea without action is worthless.

Many times taking action can produce mistakes. Take mistakes as an important step or investment in your education. Avoid them by thinking the plan and your desired scenario through. Learn from them. And never again repeat them. When you were a kid and you practiced walking, you fell. And I am sure that you fell more than once. Several times, again and again. And what did your parents do? They celebrated every small step you made, but also your falls. But you were falling and in some way even failing to walk, but you were encouraged to repeat and practice walking again and again.

> MANY TIMES TAKING ACTION CAN PRODUCE MISTAKES. TAKE MISTAKES AS AN IMPORTANT STEP OR INVESTMENT IN YOUR EDUCATION. AVOID THEM BY THINKING THE PLAN AND YOUR DESIRED SCENARIO THROUGH. LEARN FROM THEM. AND NEVER AGAIN REPEAT THEM.

After all that trial and error, you learned how to walk and you have done it since the early days of your life. You took action, lots of action and lots of mistakes before you mastered it. Richard Branson wrote: "You don't learn to walk by following rules. You learn by doing, and by falling over."

Self-made millionaires that I have studied have probably made more mistakes in their lives than anyone else. Many of them have gone bankrupt, some of them even more than once. Some of them have committed some legal misconduct and learned from it and grown to do business ethically; some of them have even lost their businesses entirely and managed to rebuild them, growing even stronger and smarter. The ritual of putting passion into what they do is a very important ritual of self-made millionaires.

STUDYING THEIR STORIES AND THE OBSTACLES THEY ENCOUNTERED LED ME TO A SIMPLE CONCLUSION. SELF-MADE MILLIONAIRES AND SUCCESSFUL PEOPLE TAKE HEARTY ACTION ON A DAILY BASIS.

Studying their stories and the obstacles they encountered led me to a simple conclusion. Self-made millionaires and successful people take hearty action on a daily basis. One of my students, and one of the best swimmers in the world, told me that he had his vision for the gold medal in his mind every morning when he woke at five a.m. on a cold winter day, drove to the gym, and at six a.m. he was in the cold water, swimming. Some days his entire body hurt, it was freezing when he jumped into the water. But he did it, he took action with all his heart every single day, because he had in his mind a clear goal or a vision with every practice he did. Use ritual number one to have heartier, passionate action. Visualize clearly where you want to go. If they did not have a great passion and great faith in who they are and what they do, which I named hearty passion, most self-made millionaires would simply quit. Many times, self-made millionaires did not know how to survive one month to the other. They had literally nothing, or worse, they had a huge debt and went bankrupt, or sometimes became quite close bankruptcy. But the passion for what they do made them come back. The passion for what they do, coming from their hearts or from loving what they do, or simply something inside of them allowed them to pursue their goal and move forward and fight.

> SELF-MADE MILLIONAIRES DID NOT KNOW HOW TO SURVIVE ONE MONTH TO THE OTHER. THEY HAD LITERALLY NOTHING, OR WORSE, THEY HAD A HUGE DEBT AND WENT BANKRUPT, OR SOMETIMES BECAME QUITE CLOSE BANKRUPTCY. BUT THE PASSION FOR WHAT THEY DO MADE THEM COME BACK.

Passion comes out of powerful beliefs in what we do and powerful beliefs of who we are. Beliefs are just ideas that we have about the world, about others and about ourselves. Self-made millionaires have very powerful beliefs about themselves and about their products and services. The beliefs that they have are many times more powerful than any average observer would think. But those beliefs, along with their faith, help them to persist and act. The hope that they have inside of them allows them, in the moments of their great challenges, to be persistent and determined to push ahead. You can build more beliefs and more hope by reading this book several times, by reading great inspiring books several times, using affirmations, incantations, reading your goals aloud with passion, reading your goals and moving, jumping, dancing to some great music, etc. When you do all that, you will increase your faith, influence your beliefs and feel your body with more energy to take action. Create a ritual in your life where you take action with great passion towards the achievement of your goal.

Set your own standards when you do that, raise the bar and the standards to achieve what you would like to achieve in your life by taking action. Become a man or woman of action, not of words. Some people speak about it, self-made millionaires do it, and in everyday life. If you speak about how much you would like to plant the flowers, visualize the process and look for motivation; the flowers will not grow in your garden without action. But if you take action, you can expect results. Often, self-made millionaires did not know how they would do it and were not sure that the direction in which they were going correct, but by taking action they learned and were able to change the course towards the direction that would most likely bring the desired results. Bringing results into life is always based on inspired and hearty action from consciously and unconsciously moving in the same direction, being in balance.

CREATE A RITUAL IN YOUR LIFE WHERE YOU TAKE ACTION WITH GREAT PASSION TOWARDS THE ACHIEVEMENT OF YOUR GOAL.

When you know where you want to go, create a plan. Make a one year, two year, three year or even five year plans. Use some estimated or planned numbers; think about your best case and worst case scenarios. Look for the balance in your

life. When people are not in balance, and take action without doing their homework, do not study
all the variables, invest with borrowed money, or take action for the
wrong reasons, these activities can
cause them harm. Acting from fear,
greed, depression or any other negative emotion or state might lead to

BRINGING RESULTS INTO
LIFE IS ALWAYS BASED ON
INSPIRED AND HEARTY
ACTION FROM
CONSCIOUSLY AND
UNCONSCIOUSLY MOVING
IN THE SAME DIRECTION,
BEING IN BALANCE.

one in the wrong direction. You will consciously go in one direction and unconsciously in another direction. Another example of taking action, but at the same time playing it safe, is
to become an investor. But you not do it for real, at first. Start
investing in your mind, mentally putting money on particular stocks, bonds, or derivatives and learning without risking
any real money. And when you have learned enough, then
you can start doing it for real. You will build self-confidence,
discipline and knowledge before you have risked any of your
own money. You can also practice taking "virtual" action in
other areas, so that you first learn at no cost. And do not wor-
ry about missing out on an opportunity. Richard Branson describes business opportunities as buses, there is always another one coming. You might use some self-coaching questions, which can help you evaluate your decision from different points of view. I always like the idea of asking myself
a question. When I set a goal, such as attaining ritual number
1, why do I want it? What would it bring to me? How is that
congruent with my vision, with all seven of my rituals?

A person who is taking passionate hearty action, but moving in the wrong direction, or making stupid moves, thinking

out of greed, anger, envy, being out of balance and still taking action, it can be dangerous for that person, but also to other people that surround that person. A friend of mine sometimes says that a motivated idiot is more dangerous than a non-motivated one. And in the pursuit of becoming a self-made millionaire, it is even truer. So take action with all your heart and remember to be careful and learn, and grow, and look toward doing the right thing for the right reason. Consult with experts, using some of the de-cision-making processes that are available on the Internet. Think of backup scenarios, but have a clear goal in your all the time. Great mind programming, or setting the direction, needs to include your direction, so that ritual number 1 is in your mind as much as possible.

A PERSON WHO IS TAKING PASSIONATE HEARTY ACTION, BUT MOVING IN THE WRONG DIRECTION, OR MAKING STUPID MOVES, THINKING OUT OF GREED, ANGER, ENVY, BEING OUT OF BALANCE AND STILL TAKING ACTION, IT CAN BE DANGEROUS FOR THAT PERSON, BUT ALSO TO OTHER PEOPLE THAT SURROUND THAT PERSON.

You can enhance your passion by visualizing your goal, us-ing ritual number 1, by affirmations, incantations, by prom-ising yourself that you will do whatever it takes, with every fiber of your being, to achieve that goal or direction. Passion comes more easily when you are healthy, vibrant, and full of energy. I cannot imagine that you would work long hours, for many years to come, enjoy it, have fun while doing all that, and not have the energy for passion. Eat healthily, exercise, drink plenty of water, sleep well, take good care of your body, do all the necessary things for you to be healthy and energetic;

for taking action towards your goals with hearty passion you will need all that energy. Energy is your fuel and the more energy you have, the more hearty, passionate action you can take.

EAT HEALTHILY, EXERCISE, DRINK PLENTY OF WATER, SLEEP WELL, TAKE GOOD CARE OF YOUR BODY, DO ALL THE NECESSARY THINGS FOR YOU TO BE HEALTHY AND ENERGETIC; FOR TAKING ACTION TOWARDS YOUR GOALS WITH HEARTY PASSION YOU WILL NEED ALL THAT ENERGY.

And your customers, your co-workers, the universe will notice the difference. Think of two sales people; one is selling with hearty passion and one is selling because he or she needs money to pay the bills and is waiting to get a better job. Who do you think is going to do a better job? I know that the way I put it is so obvious, but how much love, passion, dedication and action on a daily basis do you put into your product or service? An athlete trains every single day for four years to get a chance to compete at the Olympics. He trains for years to perform for a few minutes. So much hearty, passionate action to achieve a desired result. To this point, my greatest belief is that if you have hearty passion for what you do, and you take action out of that positive state, that is the biggest possible competitive advantage you can have.

Figure 4: HEARTY, PASSIONATE ACTION RITUAL

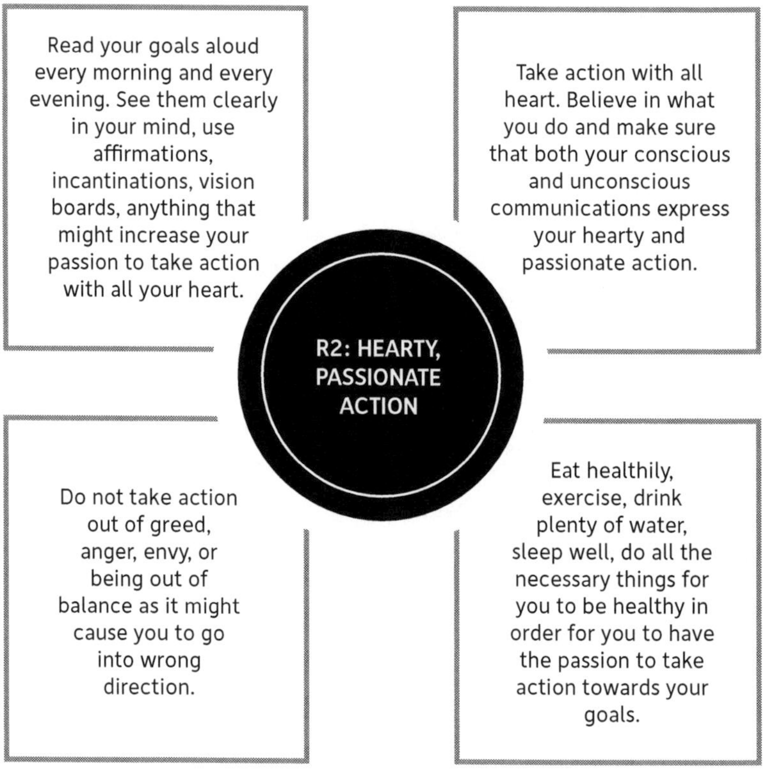

Read your goals aloud every morning and every evening. See them clearly in your mind, use affirmations, incantations, vision boards, anything that might increase your passion to take action with all your heart.

Take action with all heart. Believe in what you do and make sure that both your conscious and unconscious communications express your hearty and passionate action.

R2: HEARTY, PASSIONATE ACTION

Do not take action out of greed, anger, envy, or being out of balance as it might cause you to go into wrong direction.

Eat healthily, exercise, drink plenty of water, sleep well, do all the necessary things for you to be healthy in order for you to have the passion to take action towards your goals.

SELF ASSESSMENT QUESTIONS – YOUR MILLIONAIRE METER FOR RITUAL NUMBER 2, HEARTY PASSION:

- How much passion do you put into what you do?
- How much do you believe in what you do?
- How much do you believe in your product or service?
- How much energy do your colleagues and customers see from you?
- How could you increase your passion even more?
- How much passionate action do you take every single day towards the achievement of your goals?
- How would you like to live your dream life?
- What would you do with all the riches in your life?
- How would the people that love you show pride in you for your success?
- How much passion and energy do you put in the very important daily process of writing down and reading aloud your goals each and every day? Does the universe believe that you are serious about it?

TIPS THAT CAN HELP YOU BECOME A MILLIONAIRE BY YOUR HEARTY PASSION:

- Be passionate about what you do!
- Put your whole heart into what you do.
- You can do it, believe. Believe with passion.
- Read inspirational stories about people who are passionate about what they do.
- Make this ritual your own ritual, start now, today, immediately.
- Eat healthily, get enough sleep, think positive thoughts.

SELF-MADE MILLIONAIRE IMPLEMENTATION LIST TO DO

After you read this chapter, think of how you can take more action, what are you going to do to have more passion, to have more faith in your actions. Who is going to help you improve ritual number 2 and how are you going to bring this ritual into becoming a part of your unconscious competence? What is your first step and when are you going to do it? What are the steps that will follow?

SELF-MADE MILLIONAIRE IMPLEMENTATION LIST TO DO

What are you going to do?	By when?	Your accountability partner

*It's never crowded
along the extra mile.*

WAYNE DYER

RITUAL 3: EXTRA MILE

Ritual number one is about having a clear direction in which you want to go; ritual number 2 is taking action toward that direction, and ritual number 3 is about going the extra mile, going in that direction in a much more determined fashion than is expected and providing our services to exceed customer expectations. The extra mile ritual is to do or deliver more than we are paid for, for doing more for our customers than is expected or for doing more than our employers expect from us. If you would like to become a self-made millionaire and work normal office hours it might be theoretically possible. To increase the likelihood, I would encourage you to implement ritual number 3, to go the extra mile. Based on hundreds of self-made millionaires that I have studied, and for some of them I was fortunate enough to have details such as their working hours, all of them worked really hard. Self-made millionaires went the extra mile in time, energy, and money invested in their businesses. That does not mean that

> THE EXTRA MILE RITUAL IS TO DO OR DELIVER MORE THAN WE ARE PAID FOR, FOR DOING MORE FOR OUR CUSTOMERS THAN IS EXPECTED OR FOR DOING MORE THAN OUR EMPLOYERS EXPECT FROM US.

they did not take time off or that they didn't have hobbies or time for the families. They knew how to have fun and took time for themselves, but going the extra mile is a ritual known to most if not to all of them. Going the extra mile is one of the incredibly powerful concepts and rituals to integrate into your life if you would seriously like to become a self-made millionaire.

SELF-MADE MILLIONAIRES WENT THE EXTRA MILE IN TIME, ENERGY, AND MONEY INVESTED IN THEIR BUSINESSES.

Information about going the extra mile can also be found in the classic book from Napoleon Hill, *Think and Grow Rich*. Napoleon Hill wrote about the importance of going an extra mile. In my research I discovered that the ritual is as important, or even more important, than Napoleon Hill mentioned. Going the extra mile will highly increase your chances and your opportunities for reaching the self-made millionaire milestone. The extra mile ritual will give you all the necessary advantages against competition, and also give you one of the best warranties that the new millennium or new era can give you for your financial stability. Since I introduced this ritual into my life, my business career improved exponentially. It was amazing how clients responded. As with all the rituals, the extra mile ritual needs to be introduced with care and

GOING THE EXTRA MILE WILL HIGHLY INCREASE YOUR CHANCES AND YOUR OPPORTUNITIES FOR REACHING THE SELF-MADE MILLIONAIRE MILESTONE.

in keeping balance in your life, having time for your health, family and other activities, but still investing more time, energy and sometimes even money than one is willing to invest to simply pass through.

One of my businesses consists of personal development, motivational training, and mind programming. It is my hobby, my passion, and I also believe my life's purpose. I love training and working with clients individually. One of my students was the mother of a young man who had some problems with drugs and was associating with unpleasant friends. She asked me if I could work with him and after a few sessions with him, he stopped hanging out with them. He went back to school and found himself a part time job. I rarely work individually with clients due to my really busy schedule in running my businesses, training or writing books. However, I found time to work with him even during lunch times. After helping her son, and by going the extra mile (I needed to find time in the evenings or during lunch breaks), she became my best marketing investment. She spoke to all the people that she knew with such passion and pride and praise about my work that she brought many people to my seminars. And I never asked her to do it. All, of course, then resulted in an increased bottom line, as well. I got more and more students into my trainings and into my workshops. They continued to buy products and services from me, and many became loyal customers. I have more loyal customers when I go an extra mile. And let's be realistic; you do not need to be something that you are not when going the extra mile. I often emphasize that with all my broad knowledge of mind programming techniques, I remain a human and my friends and students often help me, they inspire me and I learn from them all the time.

I HAVE MORE LOYAL CUSTOMERS WHEN I GO AN EXTRA MILE.

If you are in a job and you would like to get promoted or

get a pay raise, do more work than you are paid for. Go the extra mile. Go the extra mile without expecting something in return, as if it is the most natural thing to do; the results show that extra payments always follow. It might not be at that very moment, it might not be in that particular job. So focus first on doing what you are expected to do, and then do some more. Remember that many great football, basketball or other sports performance people, even though they were already achieving many victories, being rich beyond all possible means, were still pushing themselves to train more and practicing some more free shots after they were already done with a regular workout or practice. Do what you do best, and do it with passion, but also go the extra mile by giving your customers or colleagues at work more than they are expecting and enjoy doing it. Do it with a nice, sincere big smile. You will become indispensable. In the new millennium, businesses and individuals have the greatest bargaining and buying power than was possible anytime in the past. There is so much choice and variety that customers can switch to another company or another supplier in seconds. By going the extra mile, you have the best recipe for customer satisfaction and loyalty, or your long term promotion, or long term employment that one can have. Having said

> GO THE EXTRA MILE WITHOUT EXPECTING SOMETHING IN RETURN, AS IF IT IS THE MOST NATURAL THING TO DO; THE RESULTS SHOW THAT EXTRA PAYMENTS ALWAYS FOLLOW.

> BY GOING THE EXTRA MILE, YOU HAVE THE BEST RECIPE FOR CUSTOMER SATISFACTION AND LOYALTY, OR YOUR LONG TERM PROMOTION, OR LONG TERM EMPLOYMENT THAT ONE CAN HAVE.

that, you still need to put a value on your time, you need to value who you are as a person and after you read all those books (including this one) and studied so many different things, you deserve to get fair compensation for your investment.

To build customer loyalty, to have customers coming back to us again and again, to actually grow long

> THINK OF WHAT YOUR CUSTOMER IS REALLY BUYING AND HOW COULD YOU GIVE THAT CUSTOMER MORE VALUE OR MORE SERVICE, WHILE AT THE SAME TIME NOT INCREASING YOUR COSTS OR YOUR WORK LOAD.

term and have safety and security in our business and in providing our personal services or business services, we need to build a ritual of going the extra mile. In the service industry, going the extra mile could mean giving small surprises to customers to build a great customer experience. It is the same with products. We focus on never-ending improvement. We focus on improving our product or service to create the best possible experience and best possible value for our customers. Study your customer well. Think of what your customer is really buying and how could you give that customer more value or more service, while at the same time not increasing your costs or your work load. Of course you are looking at your balance sheet, as you do not want to increase your costs drastically. If you are selling shampoo, you cannot give a free computer or a free car with every shampoo bottle you sell, but you might write an inspiring thought on each of the bottles or create an online community where people exchange ideas on how to use that shampoo, etc.

In the old days, ritual number 3, going the extra mile, can also be described as working harder and harder, taking ex-

treme action. Working hard is a ritual that fits into this cat-
egory. You could already talk about it with its ritual number
and say taking passionate, hearty action. Working even harder, going the extra mile, doing more than you are being paid
for, looking for something more we can offer the customer,
improving the customer experience, looking for ways to reinvent and recreate what is perceived to be the actual value, and
adding that value to the extent that the customer would be our
loyal customer, can help you substantially increase your likelihood of becoming a self-made millionaire. Working harder
when you love to do something does not really feel like hard
work at all. So going the extra mile when you love what you
do can be lots of fun. Some of the self-made millionaires that I
have met were already retired, but they told me that they love
coming to work every day because that business gives meaning to their life. And they will not consider selling the company and then playing golf or spending time on their yacht.
They love what they do and going the extra mile is actually
doing more of what they really love. It is fun. So when I meet
young people in my workshops who say that they are working in their company because they will sell it in two years,
and that they work for the sake of money, I understand the

difference and many times I can
predict how well they will do and
after some years, that prediction
comes true. For them, going the
extra mile does not come naturally. But you build customer loyalty when you provide more to
your customers. And continue to

**WORKING HARDER WHEN
YOU LOVE TO DO
SOMETHING DOES NOT
REALLY FEEL LIKE HARD
WORK AT ALL. SO GOING
THE EXTRA MILE WHEN
YOU LOVE WHAT YOU DO
CAN BE LOTS OF FUN.**

think about ritual number 3 all the time, because loyalty is not for life. We will continue to have the loyalty while we continue to give extra value and that extra mile. Bitching and moaning when going the extra mile or expecting immediate pay off, does not really help. So when going the extra mile, remember to smile, remember to have faith that all extra miles result in something that one day will be monetized, or will be paid back in another form that will benefit you.

All the self-made millionaires that I studied and met were crazy about improving. Improving and optimizing themselves and improving and optimizing their product and service. Many of them were constantly studying. Studying about what they do, or studying and practicing how to do what they do even better. Write down in a special notebook how and what to improve, based on customer feedback, talk to people and ask them about their customer experience, find out about problems that you or your product can help them solve. And then actually implement those improvements. That is the meaning of the extra mile. The extra mile ritual can be found easily in the self-made millionaires' dedication and determination to improve what they do and also to learn more and

SO WHEN GOING THE EXTRA MILE, REMEMBER TO SMILE, REMEMBER TO HAVE FAITH THAT ALL EXTRA MILES RESULT IN SOMETHING THAT ONE DAY WILL BE MONETIZED, OR WILL BE PAID BACK IN ANOTHER FORM THAT WILL BENEFIT YOU.

THE EXTRA MILE RITUAL CAN BE FOUND EASILY IN THE SELF-MADE MILLIONAIRES' DEDICATION AND DETERMINATION TO IMPROVE WHAT THEY DO AND ALSO TO LEARN MORE AND MORE.

more. I was modeling one of the self-made millionaires that owns a large production plant and it amazed me how natural it is for him to invest and reinvest more and more money

SELF-MADE MILLIONAIRES STUDY HARD AND LEARN TO IMPROVE ALL THE TIME.

into products and services that his company produces. His passion for never-ending improvement and learning how to do things better was a great inspiration. Many of the speakers and several books describe how important it is to think positively, to visualize, and things will come into our life easily and quickly, without much effort. The truth that I discovered is that self-made millionaires study hard and learn to improve all the time. You can study and improve instead of losing too much time watching TV, reading emails, cruising the Internet, and playing with social media. Think of how you can turn your spare time into building new skills and knowledge. You can study while you drive by listening to audio books, you can even study while you sleep with a special technology, you can form study groups, etc. Going the extra mile when you love what you do is not too much effort; it comes so naturally and self-made millionaires do it with passion. The extra mile does not mean you need to invest more money than you will get back in the period when you need it back. Do not connect positive or wishful thinking with being stupid and ignoring studying, rational thinking and some common sense. Look at what is working well in your life and in the lives of other people. Keep a positive and optimistic millionaire mental attitude at all times, but be in touch with reality. Keep going the extra mile by studying, learning, and practicing; but also go the extra mile by looking at the balance sheet and controlling the cash flow.

You do not need to learn the business of investing, but when you create lots of additional cash in your business, you might not see the need to invest it back into your business. Learning how to invest might be a valuable lesson, which can be an important asset. Going the extra mile can mean that you know more about investing and money. In the next chapter you will learn the importance of staying in line, which means that most of the self-made millionaires reinvested the money in their own business, or in what they do as their core business. Some people, like Warren Buffett or Richard Branson, invested by buying different businesses and applying their principles there. However, some knowledge as an investor will help you grow your business even better. Alternatively if you do not wish to learn, hire someone that can help you. But hire someone that is knowledgeable about what he teaches. The purpose of this book is not to teach you investing. Warren Buffett said, "I am a better investor because I am a businessman and I am a better businessman because I am an investor." Learn from the material you can find about him and his principles online, read books about him or other people and use that knowledge to help you to know more. But going the extra mile, learning more than is expected and necessary in this particular field, is simply expanding your basic knowledge into the field that can help you become a better businessman or entrepreneur. And you do not need to become a professional investor, I am sure that the knowledge will help you run your business better. So practice learning best practices. And practice them, as well.

Going the extra mile requires lots of practice, more than the average. Can you think of a piano player that would play the piano a few times and then simply visualize playing it, do lots of affirmations, write down his goals and become a master of it? Of course not; one needs to practice, practice, practice. Take hearty and passionate action, as we mentioned, but also go an extra mile in becoming

TAKE HEARTY AND PASSIONATE ACTION, AS WE MENTIONED, BUT ALSO GO AN EXTRA MILE IN BECOMING THE BEST YOU CAN BE, THE BEST IN THE WHOLE WORLD.

the best you can be, the best in the whole world. A great piano player would play piano several hours every single day for years, or even decades, in order to play masterfully. And he or she would love improving, learning, going the extra mile, by practicing more than the minimum. The piano player would set large goals and go the extra mile when needed to master the skills and learn as much as possible to achieve them. Many self-made millionaires wanted to be the best in the entire world or their product or service to be the best, the cheapest, the best known, the most used, etc. And they went the extra mile to master what they do to become better and better every day.

In his desire to build up Microsoft, Bill Gates spent many nights working in the office and was even found sleeping on the floor when staff came to work in the morning. His desire was so strong that he was willing to put the extra mile ritual in place. He wanted to go the extra mile to create something special and to provide the world with an operating system for every computer. He could have stopped much, much earlier, but he continued to create and went the extra mile. His willingness to go the extra mile allowed him to become one of the richest men on this planet that had ever lived. Steve

Jobs was rich beyond all human possibility at a very young age, and if becoming a self-made millionaire would have been his ultimate goal, he would have quit in his twenties. But he continued on again and again, creating new products and services, failing several times, but he continued to go the extra mile. At the end, he finally succeeded and changed the world with his products, services and a completely new philosophy about how we use phones and computers. The products and services that were created by him and his team are great proof of what going the extra mile can mean.

His products not only produced an incredible customer experience, but also showed that he and his team went an extra mile to create incredible devices, which completely changed the world of music, phones, and computing as well as many other areas. Most of the competing products that were built later on did not provide nearly as good a customer experience that his products did. The riches that he created and were still being created after his death were unbelievable. His products and solutions have revolutionized the world and the market. And going the extra mile is easier when you know why. Steve Jobs could have stopped a long time ago. Or he could have worked a few hours each day. Or he could have become average. Instead, he persisted and went for excellence, and he went the extra mile even when he got fired from his own company. Going the extra mile is a ritual that can be easily applied when you know why you do what you do. This ritual has helped to produce most of the self-made

GOING THE EXTRA MILE IS A RITUAL THAT CAN BE EASILY APPLIED WHEN YOU KNOW WHY YOU DO WHAT YOU DO. THIS RITUAL HAS HELPED TO PRODUCE MOST OF THE SELF-MADE MILLIONAIRES.

millionaires. This is a ritual that could substantially increase the likelihood of your success. Think about it, adjust it to your particular situation and go for it. In the next ritual, we are connecting the ritual of going the extra mile a ritual called 'staying in line.' This ritual requires perfection, excellence, and being the best you can be.

Figure 5: EXTRA MILE RITUAL

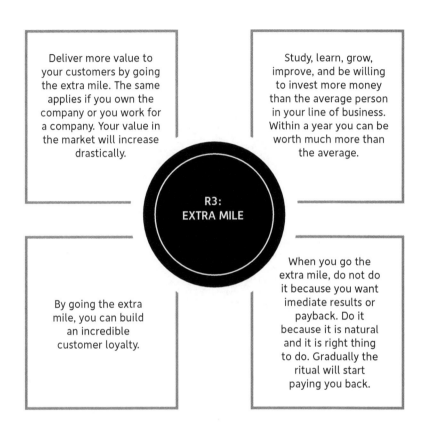

Deliver more value to your customers by going the extra mile. The same applies if you own the company or you work for a company. Your value in the market will increase drastically.

Study, learn, grow, improve, and be willing to invest more money than the average person in your line of business. Within a year you can be worth much more than the average.

**R3:
EXTRA MILE**

By going the extra mile, you can build an incredible customer loyalty.

When you go the extra mile, do not do it because you want imediate results or payback. Do it because it is natural and it is right thing to do. Gradually the ritual will start paying you back.

SELF ASSESSMENT QUESTIONS – YOUR MILLIONAIRE METER FOR RITUAL NUMBER 3, GOING THE EXTRA MILE:

- How many times do you actually go an extra mile in your life?
- Do you give your customers the best possible experience?
- How could you increase your customer satisfaction and experience even more?
- What else could you do to build a "forever" customer loyalty?
- If you could give 50 percent more, what would you do?
- How could you increase your ability to go the extra mile?
- How could you introduce a constant and never ending improvement in what you do?

TIPS THAT CAN HELP YOU BECOME A MILLIONAIRE BY GOING THE EXTRA MILE:

- Always think how to improve your customer experience!

- Ask your customers many questions about how they feel with your products and services.

- Also ask questions about what makes your customers unhappy about your products and services, or the competitors' products or services.

- Study the competition and look for any sign of them going the extra mile and note how you could go even further.

- Go for the best – never settle for less – in customer experience.

- Read inspirational stories about people who achieved the impossible, who went the extra mile in sports, business, health or any other field.

SELF-MADE MILLIONAIRE IMPLEMENTATION LIST TO DO

How can you go the extra mile with your products and services? Who can you learn from? What are you going to introduce into your life and career to go the extra mile? Think of all the activities in which you can go the extra mile and it will not affect the costs. What small things can you do to introduce the extra mile ritual? How can you build lifelong customer loyalty? Write your answers down and make sure you have an accountability partner.

SELF-MADE MILLIONAIRE IMPLEMENTATION LIST TO DO

What are you going to do?	By when?	Your accountability partner

How you start is important, very important, but in the end it is how you finish that counts. It is easier to be a self-starter than a self-finisher. The victor in the race is not the one who dashes off swiftest, but the one who leads at the finish. In the race for success, speed is less important than stamina. The sticker outlasts the sprinter in life's race.

- B. C. FORBES

RITUAL 4:
STAY IN LINE

Andrew Carnegie, a self made multi-millionaire, emphasized that the men who have succeeded are men who have chosen one line and stuck to it. If you remember Michael Jordan, when he stepped out of his line for one year, he retired from basketball to play baseball. He went out of the line and was not nearly as successful as he was in basketball. After he came back in line he again did great. Sometimes getting out of the line might take much longer to get back in again. Staying in line requires that sometimes we accept failure as part of the game, or we do not even call it failure, just feedback. Michael Jordan and all the other athletes that we admire have failed again and again, but stayed in line, and that was the reason they succeeded. In the business world, it might be harder to go back in line, so remember to stay there. Can you imagine an athlete that would train for twenty years, then won an Olympic medal in distance running, and then decided to go for rowing at the next Olympics and to skiing at the following Olympics? It sounds ridiculous doesn't it? It takes so much time to develop a competitive advantage, something really big and special. We know that people ski for several years, to be able to compete at the highest possible level. Switching lines because it is boring, or because it is not amusing, or because the neighboring business is

STAYING IN LINE REQUIRES PATIENCE, BUT ALSO FOCUS, AND GREAT COMMITMENT TO MAKE SMALL INCREMENTAL CHANGES.

presumed to be more profitable, is how some people act in their business life. And sometimes they do it even more impatiently and radically.

Staying in line requires patience, but also focus, and great commitment to make small incremental changes. Learning to stay in line from people that are self-made millionaires was one of the most important lessons of all. You have to focus on what you do well, on what brings you added value, and eliminate the rest. Do not try any new experiments in completely new fields, doing something that you know nothing about. From a distance, it might look simple. Even when self-made millionaires, or other people, who went into another line succeeded, they studied hard and learned a lot before they put their money there. Staying in line has several meanings. One of the most important is to continue growing and investing energy and time in the business that you are now in. Staying focused. Many times people see the positive side and the ease of the neighbor's business from a distance, and that tells them they should go into the neighbor's line.

Too many self-made millionaires, instead of investing and building their own businesses, invested in the stock market, where they knew nothing, or had little knowledge; it proved to be a wrong decision, which cost them much money. Greed, over-excitement, and decisions based on other people's opinions are all signs of us getting out of the line. For example, sometimes our friends, or people we trust, can have new investment ideas that they have no real knowledge about. Warren Buffet's saying had two simple rules: "Rule No. 1: Never lose money. Rule No. 2: Never forget rule No.1." When we stay in line or do what we do best, those simple rules are more easily applied. If you have owned a business for many years, you can understand how much time, effort, thinking, and studying you brought to build up your business. And now, with a few hours of studying your neighbors business, you would consider yourself an expert and invest there? I already mentioned this in ritual number 2, but I am repeating this here. Please don't make any "big" or quick decisions until you have studied the business. But never make a quick decision with financial leverage. It simply does not fit together. Stay in your line or decide to study and learn about the new business as well as you did for yours. Staying in line does not mean that you cannot reinvent what you do, innovate, try new things, look for your passion in life, but, at the same time, do not make changes on a weekly basis, as if you could spend 30 minutes each week and become an expert in the stock market. Most successful people develop skills, rituals, competencies, social networks, which took them months, years or sometimes decades to do.

> GREED, OVER-EXCITEMENT, AND DECISIONS BASED ON OTHER PEOPLE'S OPINIONS ARE ALL SIGNS OF US GETTING OUT OF THE LINE.

> WARREN BUFFET'S SAYING HAD TWO SIMPLE RULES: "RULE NO. 1: NEVER LOSE MONEY. RULE NO. 2: NEVER FORGET RULE NO.1."

Invest time, educate yourself, mitigate risk and only then invest if you have done your risk assessment. **STAY FOCUSED ON WHAT YOU DO WELL.** Some people made money over night by going into high risk gains, but if you would like to be a millionaire for many decades, then study people who have been there for a long period of time. Stay focused on what you do well. Staying in line for Richard Branson also meant applying the principles of having fun and creating great customer experiences across several industries by using a unique brand name.

Charlie Munger once explained that the philosophy that he and his partner Warren Buffett used to buy businesses is quite simple. So simple that if they would teach it in a university they could be finished in one semester. That is what the ritual staying in line really means. Staying in line is about following simple rules, which you often already know, but also being disciplined about those simple rules. For a professional athlete, staying in line would include training hard, following a diet that would enable him or her to perform the best, having a good night's sleep, and totally focusing on performance day and night. Staying and remaining focused on what they already do well, to get that small improvement, to do it even better. Staying in line means being totally and absolutely focused on what you do well, to do that extremely, extremely well. Let me put the philosophy in my own words and the way I understood it.

One of the richest people in the world uses this philosophy – he is staying in line. **SO THE MEANING OF STAYING IN LINE ALSO INCLUDES DISCIPLINE. BE DISCIPLINED AND FOCUSED.** So the meaning of staying in line also includes discipline. Be disciplined and focused.

For Warren Buffett, one of the richest people of all time, the rules sound simple. The price must be right, and the management needs to have talent and integrity, but most importantly, as investors and new potential owners of that company, they need to understand the business and need to be able to predict how well the business would do in the following years. Many times, Munger and Buffet were questioned as about why they did not buy any of the hi-tech businesses when the market was booming like crazy. But, instead, they bought businesses they understood and could predict their growth. They stayed in line. They stayed in their circle of competence. Do what you do well and leave the rest to the other people. Even though in the times of the Internet bubble, Buffett and Munger might be criticized for not being up-to-date investors, they did not listen to public opinion. They stayed in line, and some years later after the crash, they were shown to be right. Do not listen to other people's opinion or to the media. Take time to rationally think and focus your thoughts on your own business.

IF YOU ARE IN DIRECT SALES OR IN MULTILEVEL MARKETING AND YOU ARE DOING WELL OR ABOUT TO DO WELL, STAY IN LINE. SEE YOUR LONG TERM GOAL, WHERE YOU WANT TO BE, AND EVERY MORNING WHEN YOU WAKE UP MOTIVATE YOURSELF TO PERSIST AND CONTINUE.

If you are in direct sales or in multilevel marketing and you are doing well or about to do well, stay in line. See your long term goal, where you want to be, and every morning when you wake up motivate yourself to persist and continue. If you just started, be patient. Learn from your mentors and continue staying in line. Going into another business and starting from scratch is what people that are failures often do, they will go back to the beginning of the line again and again. Anytime you have an idea of quitting, simply go back and double your work and your activities and stay in line. Exercise the first three rituals with the greatest passion possible. If you are in your own company and profession where you have been for a while, and you do well, stay in line. Invest in products and services that you know about, that bring you money and have the largest potential. Avoid investing in ventures that you are not familiar with. Your competitive advantage is that you are already in line and know the people, ways of doing business, and how to become better and better. Do not switch until you are sure you have given your best and persisted in becoming a self-made millionaire. But you need to persist for years. Push yourself to improve and become better, read more, go to workshops and seminars, improve your performance and stay in line. Listen to your heart. If your heart tells you that you are in the right line, remember to persist and put in as much passion as is humanly possible; this will give you the strength and energy to make the dreams come true.

IF YOUR HEART TELLS YOU THAT YOU ARE IN THE RIGHT LINE, REMEMBER TO PERSIST AND PUT IN AS MUCH PASSION AS IS HUMANLY POSSIBLE; THIS WILL GIVE YOU THE STRENGTH AND ENERGY TO MAKE THE DREAMS COME TRUE.

Many times people approach me asking if I would like to invest money, time or energy in their business. After losing loads of money and learning from the ritual that I found in self-made millionaires, I ask myself a simple question. If I had all the money in the world, would I want to do that? There is also a second question: Would doing that increase my current business? If both questions have a negative answer, I do not even consider learning more about that idea. I stick to what I do well and I do that with passion. Staying in the line of your business is simply continuing to do what you do, and simply improving what you do all the time. Staying in line means becoming better, being patient, growing and expanding. It means doing well what you do and leaving out all the rest. Staying in line also means staying concentrated and focused. Doing what you do well and being focused on how to do that even better. Some people consider focus or doing the same thing again and again a boring thing, but when I studied self-made millionaires it was very clear to me. Self-made millionaires are so successful only because they or their businesses do something extraordinary and they have done that for many years. In reality, being better and better over a longer period of time is what staying in line is really about. For some of them success came overnight, but that night often took many years, and for some people decades. They have a niche or a line of product and service, which they do really well and patiently improve it.

And when you focus on something, you cannot focus on

IF I HAD ALL THE MONEY IN THE WORLD, WOULD I WANT TO DO THAT?

SELF-MADE MILLIONAIRES ARE SO SUCCESSFUL ONLY BECAUSE THEY OR THEIR BUSINESSES DO SOMETHING EXTRAORDINARY AND THEY HAVE DONE THAT FOR MANY YEARS. IN REALITY, BEING BETTER AND BETTER OVER A LONGER PERIOD OF TIME IS WHAT STAYING IN LINE IS REALLY ABOUT.

anything else. Steve Jobs once said that he was proud, not only of what they had decided to do, but also what they decided not to do. In the business world we call this selection of direction, a strategy. The entire process is also called strategic thinking. You need to decide what you are going to do with your business, and at the same time, what you are not going to do. Thus, staying in one line means not staying in another line. You might change your mind based on new information you get, so leave your options open, but when you are in one line, do your very best job there. Saying no to your neighbor's crazy new idea means staying in line or following a specific strategy. A strategy is when you clearly decide what you will do and what you won't do. In my research, the self-made millionaires sometimes mentioned to me that they lost money, time and energy when they were looking at what a neighbor was doing, when they were greedy and wanted to make an easy buck, or when they invested their profits or money into some other businesses where they lacked knowledge, competence or time to think and focus, etc. And in many cases they learned from that mistake, but in some other cases they didn't and it cost them even more money, time and energy. So, invest in your line of business. Stay in line and remember to understand that the neighbor's business from a dis-

> YOU NEED TO DECIDE WHAT YOU ARE GOING TO DO WITH YOUR BUSINESS, AND AT THE SAME TIME, WHAT YOU ARE NOT GOING TO DO. THUS, STAYING IN ONE LINE MEANS NOT STAYING IN ANOTHER LINE. YOU MIGHT CHANGE YOUR MIND BASED ON NEW INFORMATION YOU GET, SO LEAVE YOUR OPTIONS OPEN, BUT WHEN YOU ARE IN ONE LINE, DO YOUR VERY BEST JOB THERE.

tance might look nice, but truly has advantages and disadvantages like yours. And if you have been working in your line of business for several years it really means that you have been in line several years, and thus, you have a competitive advantage over your competition.

THEY FOCUS ON BEING THE BEST THEY CAN BE OR SOMETIMES THE BEST ON THEIR TEAM, LEAGUE OR EVEN IN THE WORLD, IN WHAT THEY DO, AND THEY LEAVE THE REST TO THE OTHER TEAM PLAYERS.

The ritual of staying in line provides a clear line of positioning yourself or your business, which means that you experiment, you test and you invest in areas that help you grow and diversify, but also help you look for your niche or product. But again, let me give you a nice metaphor from the sports world. Perfection is another word for saying 'staying in line.' And perfection can be sometimes boring. Look at professional athletes, they usually start training when they are kids, and they do that for a couple of decades. Only then can they get some measurable and worthwhile results. Some of them do the same movement or moves again and again for ages. They stay in line. Some athletes train and prepare several hours every single day, sometimes for decades, in order to be able to compete and there is no guarantee that they will make it. They choose a specific sport, but not only that, sometimes athletes also choose a niche within that sport. In soccer, we look at goal keeper and a striker; they train and prepare differently. They focus on being the best they can be or sometimes the best on their team, league or even in the world, in what they do, and they leave the rest to the other team players.

Often, working towards perfection is demanding not only

for the athlete, but for many of the people around him or her. Remember that perfection does not mean that you will wait until there are perfect conditions on the market or with yourself, because you might need to wait for a really long time.

PERFECTION MEANS YOUR COMMITMENT TO A CONSTANT AND NEVER-ENDING IMPROVEMENT IN THE SAME AREA, SAME LINE.

Perfection means your commitment to a constant and never-ending improvement in the same area, same line. Many times, self-made millionaires are not understood, or even fought against, by their employees or other people close to them, because they strive for high quality and they strive for perfection. Only their persistence in staying in line can help them to become self-made millionaires.

When I studied self-made millionaires from direct sales and multi-level marketing companies, the common pattern is obvious. Look at millionaires within a specific company. Multi-level marketing millionaires all had a clear focus and stayed in line, they persisted when others quit or kept changing lines. It takes time to build networks, but once they build them, they can create incredible results simply by educating, motivating and supporting their members of the network and continuing to grow those networks. I have been hired by many different direct sales companies as a speaker to inspire, motivate and train their members. Sometimes I co-train with their best people. One of the guest speakers was a really and truly successful woman who broke many of the company records. Her key focus was

MULTI-LEVEL MARKETING MILLIONAIRES ALL HAD A CLEAR FOCUS AND STAYED IN LINE, THEY PERSISTED WHEN OTHERS QUIT OR KEPT CHANGING LINES.

on staying in line, focusing entirely on her business. She disregarded what other people, who knew little or nothing about the business, said and she helped all her people within her group to sell more. As they became successful she was more successful, too. Remember to help others become more successful, and you will become more successful, too.

Help, inspire and motivate your people to stay in line was what I learned from her. She stayed in line when times were difficult and motivated other people to stay in line, too. The result was that the reward was there. She won several company records. Do not allow yourself to be taken out of the line until you have given your very best. Self-made millionaires in directs sales did not switch from one company to the other. They worked hard for the same network marketing company; they worked on their network, improved their skills and worked with passion and persisted when other people quit or looked for another opportunity. Remember to practice all four rituals that we have covered so far, with all your passion and determination, and that the staying in line ritual requires patience, requires seeing the big picture and requires being fully and totally determined to make things happen. As you are, then you will definitely stay in line, you will definitely remain focused.

Remember that other people, some of whom love you dearly,

will sometimes try to take you out of your line. They will try to present you with their limiting beliefs. Some might be true, some totally untrue. Listen to your heart and follow your passion. Family and friends of people who do not even work in multi-level marketing companies, or any business you would like to work in, are the ones that suddenly turn into the most experienced business consultants on this planet and would like to talk you out of what you do. Remember to listen to their advice, but if you want to climb Mount Everest, remember that you would rather take advice from people who have climbed Mount Everest before and are experts in the field of climbing that mountain. At the end of the day, take enough time to think your decisions through thoroughly. It is great to surround yourself with people that are more experienced than you are and people that are more successful than you are. But, at the end of the day, the responsibility is yours for any decisions you will make. You are responsible for any decisions you make, therefore you should decide according to your value system and while in a positive mental state.

Taking tips and suggestions from people that are experts in what they do and are successful can be helpful, but, as we just mentioned, at the end of the day, the responsibility is yours; it is good that you still think with your head. And when looking for advice and a formula, surround yourself with self-

> **TAKE ENOUGH TIME TO THINK YOUR DECISIONS THROUGH THOROUGHLY.**

> **YOU ARE RESPONSIBLE FOR ANY DECISIONS YOU MAKE, THEREFORE YOU SHOULD DECIDE ACCORDING TO YOUR VALUE SYSTEM AND WHILE IN A POSITIVE MENTAL STATE.**

made millionaires who actually make money. They can give you practical as well as theoretical advice. And that is what this book is about. To give you some new ideas and generalized experience from people who stayed in line. The book is not about people who quit after a week, a month or a year. It is to help you think differently, when you think differently you feel differently and your actions become different. The critical and rational thinking is still yours to do. So remember to do that. Think with your own head.

If you wait in the line at a movie theatre, and you have waited for some time, you might decide that the next line is moving faster, so you switch. When you do that, you must go back to another line again, so starting all over. Switching lines will bring you to the end of the next line. It might be exciting at first, new people, perhaps new ways of acting and behaving, but you will go at the beginning of the line. This also happens in the business world when you get bored or tired of your business. You must get back in line at another business and start from beginning. Therefore, the ritual that clearly leads to success is being focused and building sales and a network with the branch or direct sales network you are in. When some people decide to switch, it is like going back to another line. Remember that most of the time people with discipline and people

SWITCHING LINES WILL BRING YOU TO THE END OF THE NEXT LINE. IT MIGHT BE EXCITING AT FIRST, NEW PEOPLE, PERHAPS NEW WAYS OF ACTING AND BEHAVING, BUT YOU WILL GO AT THE BEGINNING OF THE LINE.

MOST OF THE TIME PEOPLE WITH DISCIPLINE AND PEOPLE PATIENTLY STAYING IN LINE BEAT THE TALENT.

patiently staying in line beat the talent as talent is only the starting point. After implementing the first three rituals, it is about staying in line, being patient. In the real business world, this means that when you patiently follow the first three rituals, and stay in line, which is ritual number 4, you may discover some special miracles happening.

The majority of self-made millionaires stayed in line. They all worked hard and persisted in their niche of business. Steve Jobs did not go from computers to real estate. And Warrant Buffet did not go from investing in businesses that he understood to businesses that he could not make predictions about, such as software or computers. Simple as that. They both stayed in line. That does not mean that they

BE PREPARED TO CHANGE YOUR MIND OR TO CHANGE YOUR BELIEFS ABOUT SOMETHING BASED ON NEW INFORMATION YOU RECEIVE. SOMETIMES YOUR PRODUCT AND/OR YOUR SERVICES NEED TO CHANGE DRASTICALLY BECAUSE THE WORLD IS CHANGING. YOUR LINE CAN CHANGE OVER TIME; IT MIGHT TAKE A TURN, SO LISTEN YOUR HEART AND LISTEN TO THE MARKET.

did not study other business ventures and or that they did not listen to the market. That is actually very important. Both of them did things differently in the beginning of their careers. Be prepared to change your mind or to change your beliefs about something based on new information you receive. Sometimes your product and/or your services need to change drastically because the world is changing. Your line can change over time; it might take a turn, so listen your heart and listen to the market. But don't change your mind completely on a weekly or daily basis. Do not do it because your neighbor's wife read some information on an Internet forum and told you so, but because you have a rational thinking process in place and you did proper homework on which an important decision must be based. It is ok to admit that you were wrong a week ago, a month ago, a year ago. It is OK to switch lines because your line has reached a dead end, but do it only after a thorough and rational thinking process and for the right reasons. Some companies did not pay attention to the future of their businesses and their lines and they are no longer in the business. One of the things worth remembering is that staying in line for a long period of time can lead to excellence when the line we are in has lots of potential.

If you eventually decide that you would really like to go into another line and switch your business to another field, but you must stay in the old line for a while because you need to make some money to survive, it is okay to stay in two lines at the same time. I did it for many years, until my writing and speaking business took off. Ensure that in your current line, your current business and job, you give your very best. Continue to program your mind all the time. If you perform and give only 50 percent for the time being, you might set up some lazy patterns, which you might bring with you to the job or business of your dreams, to your dream line. Mentally, link up your dream line and

> EVEN THOUGH YOU ARE FORCED TO STAY IN NOT-SUCH-A-FANTASTIC LINE, BE GRATEFUL THAT YOU HAVE A JOB OR A BUSINESS, AND BE THERE WITH ALL YOUR HEART. WHATEVER YOU DO NOW UNCONSCIOUSLY, YOU WILL TAKE THOSE PATTERNS AND RITUALS WITH YOU INTO YOUR NEW LINE. WHAT YOU LEARN UNCONSCIOUSLY GOES WITH YOU EVERYWHERE.

your new dream business. Be passionate, using the full potential you give to the current job. Even though you are forced to stay in not-such-a-fantastic line, be grateful that you have a job or a business, and be there with all your heart. Whatever you do now unconsciously, you will take those patterns and rituals with you into your new line. What you learn unconsciously goes with you everywhere.

Have faith and patience. It is okay to drive in an older car for a while; it is okay not to have all the flashy toys at the beginning. You do not need to start with a great pile of money.

STAY IN LINE AND HAVE FUN

When you look at some of the self-made millionaires, many of them did not know how they would be able to pay the bills. They lived from month to month, but persisted and still worked hard to be the best they could be in their specialized field. When you do that for some time, you become one of the best in a particular field in your country. When you do that for a decade, you can become one of the best in the world. And there are no rules. Some self-made millionaires actually are in multiple lines, some of them came to a stage of expansion where they mastered one line, made loads of money and decided to use the same principles, same brand name, same ideas and philosophy in other businesses or other lines. But master one line first. Be very successful there. Self-made millionaires are built many times by applying this ritual. They stayed in line until the check became bigger than a million and many more millions. Stay in line and have fun, because your line is the best line, because you are in that line.

Figure 6: STAY IN LINE RITUAL

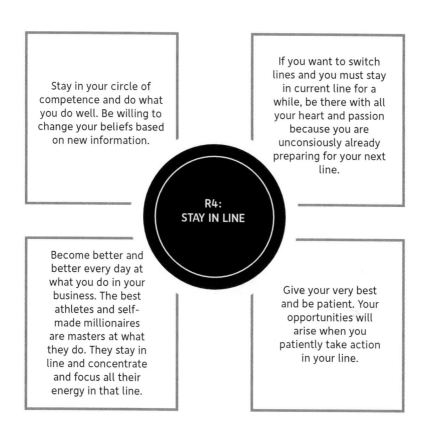

Stay in your circle of competence and do what you do well. Be willing to change your beliefs based on new information.

If you want to switch lines and you must stay in current line for a while, be there with all your heart and passion because you are unconsiously already preparing for your next line.

R4: STAY IN LINE

Become better and better every day at what you do in your business. The best athletes and self-made millionaires are masters at what they do. They stay in line and concentrate and focus all their energy in that line.

Give your very best and be patient. Your opportunities will arise when you patiently take action in your line.

SELF ASSESSMENT QUESTIONS – YOUR MILLIONAIRE METER FOR RITUAL NUMBER 4 STAYING IN LINE:

- How easily do you get bored with what you do?
- How many times did you get out of what you do best, lost money and did things that you knew wouldn't help to grow your business?
- How often do you focus on your business and work for its perfection?
- Do you strive to become the best in the world in what you do?
- How could you be even more focused at the very core of your product or service?
- What else could you do to stay in line with even more passion?

TIPS THAT CAN HELP YOU BECOME A MILLIONAIRE BY STAYING IN LINE:

- Always think about staying in line, improving your core business.

- Look at what is helping you grow and helping your business and spend money and energy in those areas that have a potential to grow.

- Do not look at the neighbor business because you might not be aware of what challenging he or she might be facing.

- Ask your customers many questions about how happy they are with your products and services.

- Also ask your customers what they are dissatisfied about with competing products.

- Go for the best – never settle for less – in customer experience.

- Read inspirational stories about people who achieved the impossible, who went their extra mile in sports, business, health or any other field.

SELF-MADE MILLIONAIRE IMPLEMENTATION LIST TO DO

Think of all the activities that you are NOT going to do and put them on your list. Think of activities that you are NOT going to invest any of your energy and money in, and be careful not to do them. Think of all the activities that will help you stay in line. What are you good at and how can you become better? Put those activities on your list and set a deadline to do them.

SELF-MADE MILLIONAIRE IMPLEMENTATION LIST TO DO

What are you going to do?	By when?	Your accountability partner

Though negotiations are a rough game, you should never allow them to become a dirty game. Once you've agreed to a deal, don't back out of it unless the other party fails to deliver as promised. Your handshake is your bond. As far as I'm concerned, a handshake is worth more than a signed contract. As an entrepreneur, a reputation for integrity is your most valuable commodity. If you try to put something over on someone, it will come back to haunt you.

VICTOR KIAM

RITUAL 5:
HONESTY AND ETHICS

Many people look at self-made millionaires and are afraid to become rich because they believe that if they want to be millionaires themselves, they need to do something dishonest. Completely untrue and the opposite. Most if not all of the self-made millionaires who have been millionaires for many years or decades are honest and ethical in business. In some minor cases, some of them did make mistakes, which mostly were never repeated. We know that Richard Branson made a small error in his early career. The authorities found that he was selling tax-exempt records domestically. After spending a night in jail and paying a huge fine, he pursued honest and ethical work. Richard Branson recommended spending a night in jail for people to learn that a good night's sleep actually matters. Modeling self-made millionaires, I have discovered that they look at doing their business long term, which requires doing it honestly and ethically. Being

MOST IF NOT ALL OF THE SELF-MADE MILLIONAIRES WHO HAVE BEEN MILLIONAIRES FOR MANY YEARS OR DECADES ARE HONEST AND ETHICAL IN BUSINESS.

RICHARD BRANSON RECOMMENDED SPENDING A NIGHT IN JAIL FOR PEOPLE TO LEARN THAT A GOOD NIGHT'S SLEEP ACTUALLY MATTERS.

honest is very important for your career. I encourage you to use the ritual number 5.

I cannot evaluate the position you are in at this very moment, but my advice for you is, if you are doing anything unethical or illegal in your private or business life, stop immediately. Decide that you stop today and start all over. If you spend time with people that do something unethical or illegal, do not do it anymore. Decide and make a clear plan. How are you going to move your life to the next level, to the level where you will do your business justly? Doing things right feels right, and doing things wrong feels wrong. It is similar to food. When you eat something that your body does not like or you overeat, your body will communicate this with you by making you feel uncomfortable. So, listen to your body if you want to eat more healthily and listen to your inner honesty system when you are making a decision. No matter where you are now, what you have done or not done, you can still make things right. Be honest, be ethical, do the right things, do the things that will make you feel good in the long run.

BE HONEST, BE ETHICAL, DO THE RIGHT THINGS, DO THE THINGS THAT WILL MAKE YOU FEEL GOOD IN THE LONG RUN.

This ritual is critical because strong ethics and honesty is helping self-made millionaires to be more creative and to be more passionate and pushing them in the right direction. A good night's sleep is a key aspect of long term and sustainable growth, and, therefore, self-made millionaires are working years and decades to build their fortune based on honesty and ethics. It is an important, crucial trait, which has helped them to build their self-esteem and self respect. It has helped them continue to work even when staying in line was not simple. Stephen M.R. Covey, the author of an excellent book, The Speed of Trust says: "The process of building trust is an interesting one, but it begins with yourself, with what I call self trust, and with your own credibility, your own trustworthiness. If you think about it, it's hard to establish trust with others if you can't trust yourself." Begin first in trusting yourself by adhering to your own values and your beliefs. Honor your word.

STEPHEN M.R. COVEY SAYS: "IF YOU THINK ABOUT IT, IT'S HARD TO ESTABLISH TRUST WITH OTHERS IF YOU CAN'T TRUST YOURSELF."

Many self-made millionaires work in a field where they do not need to sign agreements, but they honor their word, they honor what they promise, and they surround themselves with people that they can trust. Doing business in a trusted environment, which is based on honesty and ethics. Operations are quicker and simpler. They do not need to continually introduce protective procedures and mechanisms. Honor your word and maintain your reputation; it is what will keep you moving toward your goals quickly and safely. But also make sure you surround yourself with employees, partners and people that will have the same values and honesty, which will enable you to keep your reputation and good will intact. Your good name is something that will allow you to work and connect with other honorable people and self-made millionaires. Warren Buffett once

DOING BUSINESS IN A TRUSTED ENVIRONMENT, WHICH IS BASED ON HONESTY AND ETHICS. OPERATIONS ARE QUICKER AND SIMPLER.

said: "Lose money for the firm and I will be understanding, lose a shred of reputation for the firm and I will be ruthless."

Make sure that from the beginning of your career and your business honesty becomes your prime value, and that you choose people according to their integrity and your faith in them. Doing business with trustworthy people, whose word you can take for granted, is so much simpler and quicker. You know what to expect and you can trust that the other party can make your time, energy and money invested worthwhile. On the other hand, it is important that you also understand that honesty does not mean that you are unable to change your mind or change your ideas. Sometimes it can mean the opposite. If you fought for an idea, or you believed in something, but in the meantime you found more information, you could change your mind. You need to be honest and truthful with yourself and acknowledge it by changing your beliefs based on the new information. Be honest about what you believe and think. People will understand if you make mistake if you are honest with them. They won't understand and you might forever lose clients if you treat them in a dishonest way.

When Warren Buffett was asked once what he looks for in a manager, he said that he looks for intelligence, energy and integrity. He also said that if one does not have integrity, the first two will kill him. Think about how someone like Warren Buffett works with so many different managers and execu-

> MAKE SURE THAT FROM THE BEGINNING OF YOUR CAREER AND YOUR BUSINESS HONESTY BECOMES YOUR PRIME VALUE, AND THAT YOU CHOOSE PEOPLE ACCORDING TO THEIR INTEGRITY AND YOUR FAITH IN THEM.

tives. What would it look like if he could not trust them to do their job well and with integrity? Being able to trust people enables business processes to be more open and flexible. Mahatma Gandhi once said, "The moment there is suspicion about a person's motives, everything he does becomes tainted." When you have honesty in your heart and you act upon honesty people will begin to trust you and you will be able to build up long term relationships with people and sustain your business.

When you do what you love to do, you would like to do it for many years. Think about the professional athletes that are unable to compete because they have used illegal drugs to enhance their performance. To do what you love to do well, you need a good night's sleep, you need to build up your brand, and your name. Your name and your handshake can help you bring your first million with more millions to come. Decide today that you are going to be a self-made millionaire with many years to follow. Do not try to save money by not paying all of your taxes, or by not keeping your word with other people, including your suppliers and customers. If you are still unsure, imagine your decision as published in your local newspaper. How would you feel about it? When you start observing people that are self-made millionaires and have been so for a long

WHEN WARREN BUFFETT WAS ASKED ONCE WHAT HE LOOKS FOR IN A MANAGER, HE SAID THAT HE LOOKS FOR INTELLIGENCE, ENERGY AND INTEGRITY. HE ALSO SAID THAT IF ONE DOES NOT HAVE INTEGRITY, THE FIRST TWO WILL KILL HIM.

WHEN YOU HAVE HONESTY IN YOUR HEART AND YOU ACT UPON HONESTY PEOPLE WILL BEGIN TO TRUST YOU.

time, the honesty ritual is a key ritual to remember and to keep in mind.

The honesty ritual requires some patience. Sometimes there are fake opportunities in your business life that might misguide you, promising that you could get to your first million by using shortcuts. Do not go there. Stop, think it over and decide on honesty. Yes, you will certainly sleep better, you won't be risking your career and your name. In addition, you would be doing the right thing. Be honest, not only because you will sleep better, but also because it is the right thing to do. And that is the most important part of the honesty ritual. Do the right thing because it is the right thing to do, and doing the right things can lead you safely and with pride to your first million, with many more millions to follow. If you need to be patient and work longer hours to achieve your first million because you are following the honesty ritual, I would still encourage you to do so. At the end it will pay off. Honesty pays off.

BE HONEST, NOT ONLY BECAUSE YOU WILL SLEEP BETTER, BUT ALSO BECAUSE IT IS THE RIGHT THING TO DO.

Figure 7: **HONESTY AND ETHICS RITUAL**

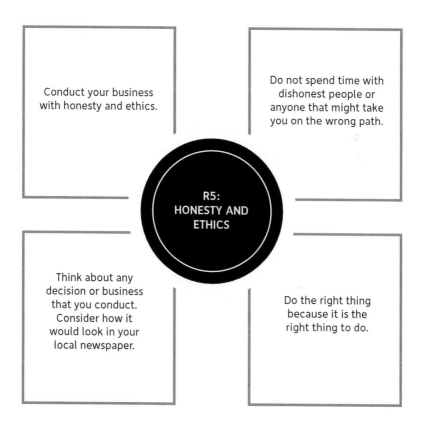

Conduct your business with honesty and ethics.

Do not spend time with dishonest people or anyone that might take you on the wrong path.

R5: HONESTY AND ETHICS

Think about any decision or business that you conduct. Consider how it would look in your local newspaper.

Do the right thing because it is the right thing to do.

SELF ASSESSMENT QUESTIONS – YOUR MILLIONAIRE METER FOR RITUAL NUMBER 5 HONESTY AND ETHICS:

- How well do you communicate honestly and openly with your colleagues?
- Do you live by the virtue 'my life is my message'?
- Is honesty and ethics one of your top three values?
- When you have a choice between making lots of money or being honest or ethical, what do you do?
- If you haven't always been honest and ethical, how could you introduce honesty and ethics as your top values?

TIPS THAT CAN HELP YOU BECOME A MILLIONAIRE BY BEING HONEST AND ETHICAL:

- Being honest and ethical is always your very best pick.
- Just follow your inner compass and do the right things for the right reasons.
- Associate and do business with honest people and people that you can trust.
- Make sure that when hiring your people honesty is one of the top three values you look for.
- Inner peace and a good night's sleep is one of the greatest riches that self-made millionaires described. Follow their advice. Be honest. And do it because it is the right thing to do.

SELF-MADE MILLIONAIRE IMPLEMENTATION LIST TO DO

How can you be more honest with yourself and with others? Which small things can you promise to do for yourself and others? Which people have led you to dishonesty and which people have helped you become more honest? What are the activities that can help you associate more with honest people and less with dishonest people? How can you grow your business and in the next 10, 20, 30 years be proud of the manner in which you conduct yourself?

SELF-MADE MILLIONAIRE IMPLEMENTATION LIST TO DO

What are you going to do?	By when?	Your accountability partner

It's better to hang out with people better than you. Pick out associates whose behavior is better than yours and you'll drift in that direction.

WARREN BUFFETT

RITUAL 6:
YOUR MASTERMIND
GROUP

The ritual of consciously spending time with people that will help us grow and become better is widely perceived and understood as one of the most important rituals. When people spend time together there are two different types of learning

WHEN WE LEARN FROM PEOPLE THAT ARE OUR ROLE MODELS, WE CAN ONLY OBSERVE A LIMITED SCOPE OR QUANTITY OF INFORMATION AT ONE TIME.

happening. One is conscious learning. We learn what we consciously observe and see. We consciously observe what we think is important based on our values or beliefs. If we value punctuality, we observe when people are on time or not. If being on time is not our primary value, we might not notice if people are late or not, or it might not bother us as much. That part of learning is certainly important. In 1956, Princeton cognitive psychologist, George A. Miller, published a paper "The Magical Number Seven, Plus or Minus Two: Some Limits on Our Capacity for Processing Information." In this paper, Miller argues that the number of objects the average person can hold in his or her working memory is 'seven, plus or minus two' chunks of information. That means that when we learn from people that are our role models, we can only observe a limited scope or quantity of information at one time. That is one of the reasons why I would highly recommend rereading the same material or viewing, again and again, some of the best video material that you have about your role models. Of course, the book, audio, or video material does not change. But you change. If you read a good book or watch an inspiring video, again and again, you will consciously pick up different things and learn more than you did the previous time.

Even more important than conscious learning is unconscious learning; this is what we learn without being consciously aware. Did you hate some of the behavior your parents used to have when you were younger? Does it ever occur to you do some of that behavior now, unconsciously? When you started to learn how to drive a car, you were learning consciously. After you had done it for many months or years, it became unconscious, so you do it more unconsciously now. When you want to learn a foreign language, one of the best ways to learn it is to be fully immersed in the language, by traveling to the country and learning it there. You pick up rhythm, words, body language and you learn language unconsciously as well as consciously. Often when we spend time with people we repeat their words, phrases, gestures, body language, and most of these things are not picked up consciously. But we also unconsciously pick up their beliefs, values, etc. Therefore spend-

> **IF YOU READ A GOOD BOOK OR WATCH AN INSPIRING VIDEO, AGAIN AND AGAIN, YOU WILL CONSCIOUSLY PICK UP DIFFERENT THINGS AND LEARN MORE THAN YOU DID THE PREVIOUS TIME.**

ing time with highly successful people can help us learn, both consciously and unconsciously.

The mastermind ritual is great for getting the right feedback from people who motivate you, rather than discourage you. Self-made millionaires will tell you to persist because they know failure. Successful people have failed many times. When you think of successful sales people, they receive rejections all the time. Entrepreneurs that finally succeed probably received more setbacks than anyone else. There are people who understand that there is no definite failure in life, only learning and feedback on how not to do things. To me, personally introducing a mastermind ritual and actually being a member of three mastermind groups at one time in my life was truly great. I could ask questions, get motivation, direction or simply enjoy spending time with great people. Many times we perceive self-made millionaires as odd people, but most of the ones that I have met and have had in my mastermind groups are really nice people. Some of them might be too much in love with what they do. They continually speak about it, and for an outsider, it might be boring. But even watching a person in love with what they do is a learning experience of its own.

Action can lead to mistakes, as we have discussed in ritual number 2. There is an anecdote about Edison inventing the light bulb. He failed ten thousand times before he finally succeeded in creating a working light bulb. And his mastermind group and his trust in what he did helped him to persist and finally succeed. If you look at each mistake and each failure as

> SPENDING TIME WITH HIGHLY SUCCESSFUL PEOPLE CAN HELP US LEARN, BOTH CONSCIOUSLY AND UNCONSCIOUSLY.

an opportunity to grow, you want to take more action. It is the same way when connecting with people. Not all people have good intentions toward us and not all people can help us become millionaires. But through the process of learning, connecting and exchanging information with people, they help us get feedback or see things from a different perspective. Feedback about us, feedback about the products and services that we provide. Associating with self-made millionaires and other people as part of our mastermind groups can help us discuss our plans, goals and visions with people that might have achieved similar goals.

ASSOCIATING WITH SELF-MADE MILLIONAIRES AND OTHER PEOPLE AS PART OF OUR MASTERMIND GROUPS CAN HELP US DISCUSS OUR PLANS, GOALS AND VISIONS WITH PEOPLE THAT MIGHT HAVE ACHIEVED SIMILAR GOALS.

Self-made millionaires have interesting, unconscious thinking and acting programs about money, because they learned how to make millions. Within mastermind groups, we can unconsciously learn those ways of thinking and acting. People express their values and beliefs with their behavior, acting on priorities and by speaking them out loud. Many times those beliefs and values are unconscious. Self-made millionaires might fiercely believe in themselves, or in the principle of never giving up. We can learn that value or belief from them. Our unconscious thinking and acting about money, about doing business or working with people can sometimes block us or lead us to self-sabotage. There are many ways we can reprogram our thoughts with a special technique or by learning new rituals. A mastermind ritual can help us learn new ways of thinking because we associate with people that think differently. The mastermind ritual is also associated with peer pressure. We do better when we promise others that keep us accountable, and we do better when we see that that others are able to do better or are moving in the direction of their goals. When you spend time with people that have been to Mount Everest and will tell you about how strong, prepared, determined they were, you will become more motivated to climb that mountain. And when they tell you about their mistakes and the lessons learned, it could enable you to bypass some mistakes and take a more secure path to get to Mount Everest, faster and safer.

When you look at the whole process of becoming a self-made millionaire, it is similar to that of climbing a mountain. You need a plan, you consult with an expert and follow through. Think of your mountain as your first million, and then,

> A MASTERMIND RITUAL CAN HELP US LEARN NEW WAYS OF THINKING BECAUSE WE ASSOCIATE WITH PEOPLE THAT THINK DIFFERENTLY. THE MASTERMIND RITUAL IS ALSO ASSOCIATED WITH PEER PRESSURE.

like most people who climb mountains, you find new peaks, new millions to make along the way. A mastermind ritual is really spending time with people who have been at the mountain before or have a passion to go there and are using their energy, their closeness, which can help you grow and learn, consciously and unconsciously, how to get there. We can get inspired by people who have fought high altitude, freezing weather, difficult conditions and managed to climb to the peak, and survive. And have done so many times. In the same way, people who are self-made millionaires, or others who inspire us due to their traits or rituals, can help you get your first million faster. Use the feedback gained within a mastermind group to improve and change.

Sometimes the best way to learn and remember is to actually learn from mistakes. It might be necessary or it might be the only way. Sometimes a mentor or a person who went through that process can help us skip a mistake. And a mentor can be used as a mastermind in the learning process. In the business world or investment world, learning from other people's mistakes might be much, much cheaper. A mentor can also offer help or advice, which you can apply easily when you want to solve a problem or fix a mistake. A mentor can be a part of a mastermind alliance, where one can seek advice, confirmation or discuss goals without being afraid of being judged or criticized. The mastermind ritual enables us to be part of a learning and mentoring environment, where one can discuss and benefit from the discussion with the mastermind alliance. Most self-made millionaires had mentors, role models or people that helped them grow.

Having said all that, it is important that you still think rationally and with your own brain. Being rational and having structure in your thinking process can help with many decisions. Rational means that you do not follow everything that people around you suggest. When you receive an expert opinion, think it through, use a structured and rational thinking

> USE THE FEEDBACK GAINED WITHIN A MASTERMIND GROUP TO IMPROVE AND CHANGE.

> A MENTOR CAN BE A PART OF A MASTERMIND ALLIANCE, WHERE ONE CAN SEEK ADVICE, CONFIRMATION OR DISCUSS GOALS WITHOUT BEING AFRAID OF BEING JUDGED OR CRITICIZED.

process and follow it up. When you receive negative feedback that might discourage you, it might be useful and important that you act as a polarity responder. Think with your head and do not allow negative feedback from other people; do not allow someone to steal your motivation. There are some things you believe in and do not allow others to challenge. Remember that you need only a few members of your mastermind alliance or heroes to support you with your thinking process. Sometimes your spouse, your best friend, or one of your parents can also be your member of the mastermind alliance. Think of the environment you would like to be surrounded with. Self-made millionaires surround themselves with people that they love spending time with, with people that share similar values and connect with them based on similar views of the world. Self-made millionaires surround themselves with highly successful people that often have more specialized knowledge than they do.

THINK WITH YOUR HEAD AND DO NOT ALLOW NEGATIVE FEEDBACK FROM OTHER PEOPLE; DO NOT ALLOW SOMEONE TO STEAL YOUR MOTIVATION.

SOMETIMES YOUR SPOUSE, YOUR BEST FRIEND, OR ONE OF YOUR PARENTS CAN ALSO BE YOUR MEMBER OF THE MASTERMIND ALLIANCE.

Self-made millionaires surround themselves with people that pushed them or were as passionate as they were and that helped them create what they wanted to create. The frequency of meeting and using the mastermind ritual is often misperceived. You can have regular, formal daily, weekly, monthly, etc. mastermind meetings. However, the mastermind ritual can also be an informal or natural process. For some people the mastermind ritual was as simple as hiring the best people that were on the market, looking for the best of the best and making sure they give their best. Having the best people on the team helped them grow and become better and better. Look for the smartest people to be included in your mastermind group as they will help you think differently, think outside your box, and grow. For some self-made millionaires this ritual meant surrounding themselves with open-minded people who were exploring and went beyond their boundaries. One self-made millionaire formed a mastermind group outside of his businesses with people who he did not directly employ or have a partnership with. They exchanged business ideas, helped grow each other businesses through a support network. The mastermind ritual comes from trusting others and understanding that everyone has some great talent. It combines that talent, forming a direction or a goal, which can produce magic, our seventh ritual.

LOOK FOR THE SMARTEST PEOPLE TO BE INCLUDED IN YOUR MASTERMIND GROUP AS THEY WILL HELP YOU THINK DIFFERENTLY, THINK OUTSIDE YOUR BOX, AND GROW.

When looking for talents that are included in someone's mastermind group, there are many different methods. At the beginning of their careers, self-made millionaires sometimes invited talented people to become co-founders of their businesses, trusting that the unique knowledge or traits that those individuals could bring would increase the likelihood of achieving their goals. Some of the self-made millionaires hired the best people to be part of their company mastermind group. At the same time, they fired people that were not good at helping them achieve their goals. One of the famous sayings of Jim Rohn, author and speaker, is: "We become the average of the five people that we spend the most time with." Is there anyone that surrounds you and can help you achieve your goals faster? Really highly successful people might be hard to hire or partner with. However, you can look at formal or informal ways of connecting to those people to be able to learn from them.

The mastermind concept and ritual is a unique form of unconscious learning of habits, rituals, values, beliefs, energy, and principles. We learn consciously from listening to people, from observing and absorbing the information, from taking notes and being focused on conscious learning. We unconsciously learn things like thinking processes, habits, behavior from our parents, teachers or friends, sometimes even the ones we do not like. And many years later we surprise ourselves by acting the same or similar way. Even when we talk to children, we want them to associate with other children that are nice. We do not want our kids going into any gangs or spending time with kids that would badly influence their behavior. The same occurs with adults and self-made millionaires. Even drivers of highly rich people many times become wealthier or smarter because of their unconscious learning by spending time with people who are very successful. Warren Buffett pursued working

> ONE OF THE FAMOUS SAYINGS OF JIM ROHN: "WE BECOME THE AVERAGE OF THE FIVE PEOPLE THAT WE SPEND THE MOST TIME WITH."

> THE MASTERMIND CONCEPT AND RITUAL IS A UNIQUE FORM OF UNCONSCIOUS LEARNING OF HABITS, RITUALS, VALUES, BELIEFS, ENERGY, AND PRINCIPLES.

and learning from his mentor, Benjamin Graham. He had spent several years trying to work for him until he finally succeeded. Think of who could be such a mentor for you and volunteer to help that mentor for free, or think of other ways how you can spend as much time as possible with that mentor.

EVEN DRIVERS OF HIGHLY RICH PEOPLE MANY TIMES BECOME WEALTHIER OR SMARTER BECAUSE OF THEIR UNCONSCIOUS LEARNING BY SPENDING TIME WITH PEOPLE WHO ARE VERY SUCCESSFUL.

And if you cannot learn face-to-face from that mentor, look at articles, books, and videos. Youtube.com is a phenomenal place to learn from the geniuses of our era.

The mastermind group, and the concepts that are necessary for making the group work, are described in the book, Think and Grow Rich, by Napoleon Hill, which I would strongly recommend. In the book, Hill wonderfully describes a mastermind group as: "The coordination of knowledge and effort of two or more people, who work toward a definite purpose, in the spirit of harmony." Seek out people that are smarter than you, that have beliefs, values, behaviors that can help you achieve your goals faster. You can do that in many different ways, from joining clubs, visiting events, connecting with social media, reading, studying, etc. The studies I have read suggest that the actual ritual of using and introducing masterminds into one's business life has been done in different ways and

THINK AND GROW RICH, BY NAPOLEON HILL, WONDERFULLY DESCRIBES A MASTERMIND GROUP AS: "THE COORDINATION OF KNOWLEDGE AND EFFORT OF TWO OR MORE PEOPLE, WHO WORK TOWARD A DEFINITE PURPOSE, IN THE SPIRIT OF HARMONY."

that there are no rules. Find your own rule and follow it.

Remember that this is a truly yet simple way of learning. It is more powerful than we can imagine. People who we spend a lot of time with influence us more than we even care to think. Their beliefs, values and strategies can become our own. Isn't a mastermind ritual a great form of personal development and growth where, by associating with great people, we can get infected with their passion, motivation, and energy? The effect of mastermind groups is even greater when two or more minds join together. In that case, we often experience a quantum leap. We have more minds thinking of a solution to a problem or thinking about how to achieve a goal. The group likely will come out with a great idea, which a single person, or several people working alone, would never be able to come to. And we can do that in a selective way when we learn consciously, focusing on a particular part of what we would like to learn from that person. One example might include being rational at investing, but not to include eating habits. However, unconscious learning might be less selective, and we might pick up wanted and unwanted habits or behavior unknowingly.

ISN'T A MASTERMIND RITUAL A GREAT FORM OF PERSONAL DEVELOPMENT AND GROWTH WHERE, BY ASSOCIATING WITH GREAT PEOPLE, WE CAN GET INFECTED WITH THEIR PASSION, MOTIVATION, AND ENERGY?

Also – we need to remember one very important thing: There is one person that we spend most of our time with – that is ourselves. We spend most of our time with our own thoughts and our own thinking

THERE IS ONE PERSON THAT WE SPEND MOST OF OUR TIME WITH – THAT IS OURSELVES.

processes. There are several exercise and several techniques that can improve our thinking processes and focus our mind to achieve better results. The most important part is to always think about the desired results. Use ritual number 1 as the ritual for figuring out what to think about. Our internal dialogue, or internal voice, should be discussing what we want to create, what we want to have, or what we want to be. We visualize or imagine what we want to achieve. We can also imagine talking to successful people or thinking how one of our role models would think, putting ourselves in other people's shoes. For example, consider what Warren Buffett would think in this particular case, the one that we are thinking of at the very moment. Once we do that we can mentally use a virtual mastermind group, which is similar to consulting with our mentors or self-made millionaires and putting ourselves in their shoes.

> A VIRTUAL MASTERMIND GROUP, WHICH IS SIMILAR TO CONSULTING WITH OUR MENTORS OR SELF-MADE MILLIONAIRES AND PUTTING OURSELVES IN THEIR SHOES.

Virtual mastermind groups can help us affect our own thinking process, which can help us involve our internal resources, or simply help us think or look at different situations or problems from a different perspective. I have introduced my virtual mastermind in my life by reading or listening to biographies or stories about people that are my role models and thus bringing their thoughts and their energy into my mind. A short list of those people can be found at the beginning of the book, but you should create your own list. Each person has their own model of the world, which has some limitations. Only use the traits that you find resource-ful and useful for your goals and current objectives in your virtual masterminds. Leave the rest out. There are people who use lots of negative motivation to achieve their goals. That is not something that would work for me, but it might work well for you. Remember that you should only look for those traits, values, beliefs and strategies that are congruent with who you are and who you would like to be.

> ONLY USE THE TRAITS THAT YOU FIND RESOURCEFUL AND USEFUL FOR YOUR GOALS AND CURRENT OBJECTIVES IN YOUR VIRTUAL MASTERMINDS. LEAVE THE REST OUT.

Having studied with NLP experts such as John and Kathleen La Valle, Paul McKenna and the co-creator of NLP, Dr. Richard Bandler, I have learned a process that can help you create a virtual mastermind, which, in the world of Neurolinguistic programming, is called Deep Trance Identification. In Deep Trance Identification or DTI, we put people in a trance and have them step into the experience of another person and completely identify with their world. This helps them to create their own virtual masterminds.

We can do this to ourselves. It is a potent process, which can be done if we simplify it by asking ourselves a powerful question: "How would my role model react in this situation?" Or, being more specific and more direct: "What possible solutions would Richard Branson have for the challenge I am facing right now?" Having done deep trance identification

> IN DEEP TRANCE IDENTIFICATION OR DTI, WE PUT PEOPLE IN A TRANCE AND HAVE THEM STEP INTO THE EXPERIENCE OF ANOTHER PERSON AND COMPLETELY IDENTIFY WITH THEIR WORLD. THIS HELPS THEM TO CREATE THEIR OWN VIRTUAL MASTERMINDS.

several times, it seems to me to be more of an intellectual experience. I say: "Well, if I were Richard Branson, I would do this and that." Other times it is more of a kinesthetic, or a feeling, experience. I feel more motivated or more confident after putting myself in the shoes of a successful person. The process of using virtual masterminds using DTI becomes more powerful after you have done it several times. I prefer to do it standing, so that I imagine the person in front of me, and then I literally step in the shoes of that person and after a while, step back into my shoes.

Self-made billionaire, Charlie Munger, a right-hand man to Warren Buffett often speculated what his hero, Benjamin Franklin, would do in a given situation. In order to create a virtual mastermind, it is highly recommended obtaining all possible reading material, videos or other material that you can find about that person. I studied Michelangelo, visited places where I could observe his work and I loved using Michelangelo as a role model and as my member of the mastermind group. I spend time reflecting how he would create what I want to create. His patience, his determination and his perfection often help me to decide to wait before I finish my writing, or to spend some time by myself preparing for a workshop. I relax, take long walks and put on

THE PROCESS OF USING VIRTUAL MASTERMINDS USING DTI BECOMES MORE POWERFUL AFTER YOU HAVE DONE IT SEVERAL TIMES.

IN ORDER TO CREATE A VIRTUAL MASTERMIND, IT IS HIGHLY RECOMMENDED OBTAINING ALL POSSIBLE READING MATERIAL, VIDEOS OR OTHER MATERIAL THAT YOU CAN FIND ABOUT THAT PERSON.

his shoes to better understand how I can improve whatever I am working on and how I can touch the lives of others more profoundly. If you spend time with people that are positive, honest, determined, creative, brave, you will unconsciously tend towards acting in those ways.

IF YOU SPEND TIME WITH PEOPLE THAT ARE POSITIVE, HONEST, DETERMINED, CREATIVE, BRAVE, YOU WILL UNCONSCIOUSLY TEND TOWARDS ACTING IN THOSE WAYS.

Figure 8: MASTERMIND GROUP RITUAL

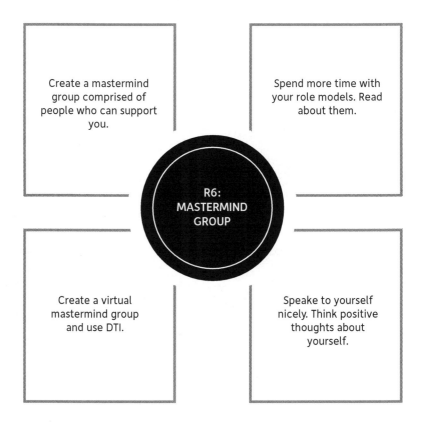

SELF ASSESSMENT QUESTIONS – YOUR MILLIONAIRE METER FOR RITUAL NUMBER 6 MASTERMIND RITUAL:

- Who do you spend the most time with?
- How often do you spend time with people who achieved what you want to achieve?
- Do you use a virtual or real mastermind concept in your life?
- Are you a member of a mastermind group that can help you become a self-made millionaire?
- Do you share your dreams with people that can inspire you and help you grow?
- Do you plan to spend more time with people that inspire you and less time with people that take the energy out of you?

TIPS THAT CAN HELP YOU BECOME A MILLIONAIRE BY USING THE MASTERMIND CONCEPT IN YOUR LIFE:

- Spend time with people that inspire you, virtually, in your thoughts and in real life.

- Associate with people that will lift your energy and will help you become a better person.

- Be yourself and be who you really are, and spend time with people that take you for who you really are.

- Read biographies and all possible information about highly successful people and self-made millionaires, and allow yourself to learn about them. Afterwards, think of how they would act in real life.

- Create your real mastermind group as well as your virtual mastermind group and put your questions and your dreams in front of them.

- Dream big and you will attract more people that can help you achieve your dreams.

SELF-MADE MILLIONAIRE IMPLEMENTATION LIST TO DO

How can you spend some time with your heroes and how can you create your mastermind group? Which activities will you undertake in order to have regular meetings with the mastermind group in your life?

SELF-MADE MILLIONAIRE IMPLEMENTATION LIST TO DO

What are you going to do?	By when?	Your accountability partner

The good news is that the moment you decide that what you know is more important than what you have been taught to believe, you will have shifted gears in your quest for abundance. Success comes from within, not from without.

RALPH WALDO EMERSON

RITUAL 7: CREATE MAGIC

Ritual number 7, creating magic is magical not only in theory, but also in practice. Let's take Steve Jobs as an example. In his mind, Jobs had many ideas. That is nothing special, is it? You and I and most of the people around us have ideas all the

THE RITUAL 'CREATE MAGIC' IS ABOUT MAKING THINGS HAPPEN. MATERIALIZING THOUGHTS. CONVERTING THOUGHTS TO SOMETHING TANGIBLE AND MEASURABLE.

time. But to make those ideas come true, to go from our minds to the material world and from there to consumers, thereby receiving a financial reward, requires many steps and some magic. Some people would say that all that is not magic, it is simply hard work, persistence and vision. And yet, many people never make it happen in spite of their hard work. Their ideas die in their heads, or worse, somebody else implements them and makes his or her millions. Steve Jobs was a master of ideas, but also a master of creating magic, so from his mind he managed to create products and services that brought billions. He created magic. The entire process, which was a ritual to him, is what I call creating magic. The ritual 'create magic' is about making things happen. Materializing thoughts. Converting thoughts to something tangible and measurable.

It could be a product or a service. And the quicker and more simple the process is from idea to results, the more we can call that process magical.

THINK ABOUT HOW YOU HAVE MATERIALIZED THOUGHTS BEFORE.

I have been studying books, millionaires and billionaires for nearly 25 years, but I still feel there are many more things for me to learn about the magic ritual. I believe in it and I believe it to be the key. And if you want a short version I would say, think about how you want your idea to change the world for the better, and how you can be a significant part of that change. Think about how you can make it happen. Let me give you some examples and some ideas about creating magic and also send you onto your path to discover how you can also create magic in your life. Think about how you have done so far, how you materialize wishes and how could become a self-made millionaire. Think of things that first were simple ideas in your life and from those simple ideas, how you made each idea become a reality. Think about how you have materialized thoughts before.

So your million, if you do not have it in your bank account yet, is simply a thought just now. If you haven't materialized your first million yet, take something simple, for example, like a glass of water. When you think of drinking that glass of water, you simply go out and make it happen. It seems so obvious. You know the strategy, you believe you can do it, and you act upon it to get it. And if you wanted a million glasses of water, you would go step by step to those million glasses of water. So you know how to materialize something simple, which a few hundred years ago it would have been a miracle to materialize it so quickly because people had to walk to a well, often not right outside their home. In some less developed countries, it is still not easy get drinking water on demand. Your goal should be to think how you can materialize and create the same magic for your millions as you are doing for other things, using the same thought processes.

For self-made millionaires this ritual and the actual materialization is often as natural as breathing. If you ask self-made millionaires how they create the magic of abundance, they will simply tell you that there is no magic. Most of them will give you a formula of a clear vision and hard work. They focus on describing one or more of the first six rituals. But then consider what happens if ritual number 7 is missing. There are people who have a vision and work really hard, but are financially broke and far from being a self–made millionaire. When you see people being passionate, knowing what they want and going the extra mile, but they do not have money in their life, look for the missing ritual. When I discovered that, and further studied self-made millionaires, I continually asked myself a question. What makes the real difference and how can I put this into a formula? What else is key to creating the magic?

YOUR GOAL SHOULD BE TO THINK HOW YOU CAN MATERIALIZE AND CREATE THE SAME MAGIC FOR YOUR MILLIONS AS YOU ARE DOING FOR OTHER THINGS, USING THE SAME THOUGHT PROCESSES.

THEN CONSIDER WHAT HAPPENS IF RITUAL NUMBER 7 IS MISSING. THERE ARE PEOPLE WHO HAVE A VISION AND WORK REALLY HARD, BUT ARE FINANCIALLY BROKE AND FAR FROM BEING A SELF–MADE MILLIONAIRE.

One simple idea about creating magic can be observed in the thinking of Viktor Frankl, a famous psychologist, who survived a concentration camp. In his book, Man's Search for Meaning, Frankl emphasized the following: "Don't aim at success—the more you aim at it and make it a target, the more you are going to miss it. For success, like happiness, cannot be pursued; it must ensue...as the unintended side effect of one's personal dedication to a course greater than oneself." Looking and being obsessed with goals is not the same as being dedicated to creating something much, much bigger than oneself. Frankl is right in his idea. The self-made millionaires that I studied had a goal: to become self-made millionaires. They would have quit after a few millions, but the truth is that they continued to play the game. They went on to create something bigger. Richard Branson says: "There is no greater thing you can do with your life and your work than follow your passions – in a way that serves the world and you."

> VIKTOR FRANKL, MAN'S SEARCH FOR MEANING: "DON'T AIM AT SUCCESS – THE MORE YOU AIM AT IT AND MAKE IT A TARGET, THE MORE YOU ARE GOING TO MISS IT. FOR SUCCESS, LIKE HAPPINESS, CANNOT BE PURSUED; IT MUST ENSUE...AS THE UNINTENDED SIDE EFFECT OF ONE'S PERSONAL DEDICATION TO A COURSE GREATER THAN ONESELF."

Creating something bigger could mean that you set a goal for your product or services, which would improve the lives of millions of people around the world, something that would bring massive value and tons of satisfaction. Your products and services should improve lives, solve problems, and enhance the quality of living for as many people as possible. The more people you can help, the more magic you can create and thus more millions could be coming your way. The creation of your millions will be automatic. Creating something bigger could mean that you would become extremely successful and a self-made millionaire. You could inspire the people you love as well as others with a simple idea, which has become successful against all odds. It might be quite motivating for some people. You could create so much good and become a major philanthropist after you make your millions. Or you might just have it all for yourself and your loved ones. Ultimately, those are only my ideas for you; you should create your own.

Creating something bigger is sometimes intangible. And we might not be sure whether we are there or not. And how do we know that the vision is big enough to create magic that would enable us to become self-made millionaires? How do we know when and how to create something bigger? And for sure that is not all there is to the magic ritual. Many companies have a big, bold vision and want to create something huge, but they do not materialize it. Therefore, this ritual was the most difficult one for me to understand. When observing and modeling self-made millionaires, I figured out that they have learned

YOUR PRODUCTS AND SERVICES SHOULD IMPROVE LIVES, SOLVE PROBLEMS, AND ENHANCE THE QUALITY OF LIVING FOR AS MANY PEOPLE AS POSSIBLE. THE MORE PEOPLE YOU CAN HELP, THE MORE MAGIC YOU CAN CREATE AND THUS MORE MILLIONS COULD BE COMING YOUR WAY.

AND HOW DO WE KNOW THAT THE VISION IS BIG ENOUGH TO CREATE MAGIC THAT WOULD ENABLE US TO BECOME SELF-MADE MILLIONAIRES?

how to create magic over a period of years. And for most of them it was not always like that. The ritual of creating magic, of manifesting in their lives what they want, only came after many defeats. They had to manage and turn around these failures, learn from them and with persistence, create more value.

Part of one of the rituals is thus: Look for something bigger than one million dollars or making a fortune for yourself. It is like the entire universe will support you and help you.

The next part of creating magic is expanding boundaries. When modeling and observing self-made millionaires, I discovered that they continually went beyond their boundaries and expanded their possibilities. They stayed in line, but, at the same time, expanded possibilities in their line. Or, they took their business model, looking at what they did well in their line and found ways in which they could do the same thing in some other line using their core competencies. In reality, this meant that their line was changing businesses. This part of the ritual requires letting go of one's ego, and using options and possibilities that are available based on rational strategic thinking. Expanding boundaries simply means allowing new possibilities, allowing new beliefs and allowing new options. Often it is called 'thinking outside of the box,' It sounds very simple, theoretically, but self-made millionaires have done exactly that, they thought outside of the box.

Ralph Waldo Emerson says that the line between failure and suc-

> **PART OF ONE OF THE RITUALS IS THUS: LOOK FOR SOMETHING BIGGER THAN ONE MILLION DOLLARS OR MAKING A FORTUNE FOR YOURSELF. IT IS LIKE THE ENTIRE UNIVERSE WILL SUPPORT YOU AND HELP YOU. THE NEXT PART OF CREATING MAGIC IS EXPANDING BOUNDARIES.**

cess is so fine that we scarcely know when we pass it; so fine that we often are on the line and do not know it; it is often hard to notice. When we create magic and make things happen, we might not even know that we are nearly there. Creating magic is, therefore, about putting all things together and crossing the line of theory and making it happen. All rituals are important, but the key ritual is the ritual of creating magic. The ritual of materializing, making things happen. If this ritual is missing, there may be no goal and, therefore, no results. This then means that there is no financial reward for our work and perseverance.

IF A SELF-MADE MILLIONAIRE WOULD LOSE ALL OF HIS OR HER MONEY AND BUSINESSES, MOST WOULD BE ABLE TO RECREATE THAT LOST WEALTH. THE MAGIC RITUAL IS IN THEM.

IF A SELF-MADE MILLIONAIRE WOULD LOSE ALL OF HIS OR HER MONEY AND BUSINESSES, MOST WOULD BE ABLE TO RECREATE THAT LOST WEALTH. THE MAGIC RITUAL IS IN THEM.

When I first presented the magic ritual to people around the world, it sounded like something esoteric or spiritual, but in reality it is not. Self-made millionaires would often fail to acknowledge the magical ritual. I can understand that as it is mostly their unconscious competence, something that they had developed over time. It comes so naturally to them that they do not think about it. If a self-made millionaire would lose all of his or her money and businesses, most would be able to recreate that lost wealth. The magic ritual is in them.

Ask yourself the following questions again: "What is the difference that makes the difference? What is the magic that can help you or anyone become a self-made millionaire? How can I create products and services, bring the final product to the customers, increase their satisfaction and make a profit?

"WHAT IS THE DIFFERENCE THAT MAKES THE DIFFERENCE? WHAT IS THE MAGIC THAT CAN HELP YOU OR ANYONE BECOME A SELF-MADE MILLIONAIRE?

Based on mathematics, the formula that we have so far observed is based on six rituals. You know what you want, you take passionate action, go the extra mile, stay in line, do your business honestly and surround yourself with the best people you can. When following those six rituals they should bring you success and your millions.

WHERE IS THE SECRET? WHERE IS THE MAGIC THAT FOR SOME IT IS POSSIBLE THAT, BY APPLYING THE SIMPLE FORMULA, THEY ARE SELF-MADE MILLIONAIRES AND OTHERS ARE NOT?

When we think of materializing or creating magic, when some people make it and some people don't, even if they have used the six rituals, we are searching for the seventh ritual, the one that really makes the difference.

Providing we use that formula, we should or become self-made millionaires after a period of time. And if you read most of the success, business or self-help oriented books you will find similar formulas and you will find the same main ingredients, more or less, depending on the author and his or her worldview. We said that looking for a bigger vision and expanding our boundaries is a starting step in the magic ritual. But does that really create value for our customers? Does that really materialize our ideas and goals? If not, where is the missing link? Where is the secret? Where is the magic that for some it is possible that, by applying the simple formula, they are self-made millionaires and others are not?

Let's explore something more. Another key ingredient. From modeling self-made millionaires, my discovery led me to believe that magic comes from decision-making. The third ingredient in creating magic is decision-making, the making of a final, disciplined and definite decision. Wouldn't now be a good time for you to decide to become a self-made million-aire? Decide for real, not a wishy-washy decision, but make a real, final and disciplined decision. For example, take something simple, like quitting smoking. Perhaps you used to smoke or had another habit that you did not like. You wanted to change that habit. In that situation you could set a clear direction – wanting to become a non-smoker. You could take passionate action, go the extra mile, stay in line, be true and honest to your-self and even surround yourself with strong people that are non-smokers to support you. But still, you might temporary fail, and you might repeat the same old smok-ing habit again.

Once you truly decide to stop smoking, then there is no way back, then people could give you ciga-rettes and you would simply say, 'no thanks.' Once you decide, and the key word is 'decision,' then it is done. It becomes so definite,

> **THE THIRD INGREDIENT IN CREATING MAGIC IS DECISION-MAKING, THE MAKING OF A FINAL, DISCIPLINED AND DEFINITE DECISION. WOULDN'T NOW BE A GOOD TIME FOR YOU TO DECIDE TO BECOME A SELF-MADE MILLIONAIRE? DECIDE FOR REAL, NOT A WISHY-WASHY DECISION, BUT MAKE A REAL, FINAL AND DISCIPLINED DECISION.**

so obvious, that sometimes people can't really remember that inner feeling that led them to smoke. People who used to be smokers and quit can easily understand what I mean by making a definite decision. If you never smoked, think of something else you were able to quit. A definite decision can be one of the key steps of your magic creation. People who decide to be self-made millionaires, but who, at the first opportunity, are no longer loyal to that decision, are similar to smokers who decide to quit in the morning and smoke again at their next coffee break.

How people make decisions vary. A definite decision means you align your conscious and unconscious mind towards a result. It is as if the doors to creating magic in your life begin to open. A decision means that both your conscious and unconscious minds go in the same direction. And that alignment is often a step toward bringing magic into your life, to materialize goals. For smoking, or any other example, perhaps you tried several times before you really decided. You decided in a moment of strength, you might even have promised someone; but, in a moment of weakness, you broke that promise. Those are called temporary decisions or promises. A promise has been broken, or a step back has been taken. At that point, a person's conscious mind wants something different from

A DEFINITE DECISION MEANS YOU ALIGN YOUR CONSCIOUS AND UNCONSCIOUS MIND TOWARDS A RESULT. IT IS AS IF THE DOORS TO CREATING MAGIC IN YOUR LIFE BEGIN TO OPEN.

BUT WHEN PEOPLE MAKE DEFINITE DECISIONS, THERE IS NO WAY BACK. THE DOORS BEHIND THEM, THE DOORS OF GOING BACK, CLOSE FOR GOOD.

their unconscious mind. When people make temporary decisions, they go one or two steps forward, get to the first barrier and quit, or one or two steps forward, and one step backwards; they go back and forth, etc.

But when people make definite decisions, there is no way back. The doors behind them, the doors of going back, close for good. Sometimes people do that when they face a challenge in their life. Some pain that makes internally says, 'enough is enough,' and just quit smoking, or any other activity, for good. The magic of creating millions is as simple as that. Once you decide, once you make a definite decision, which really means that deep down inside, you decide that you are going to follow all six rituals for creating your first million and you will create magic; then you will make it happen. When you make a definite decision, it is as if the universe becomes afraid of you or starts respecting you. It rearranges your way the doors to your fortune to open. And the path to your first million simply becomes a matter of time. The third part of creating magic is making a finite decision. Sometimes people think that if they decide, and the market gives them feedback about their product or service, that they should not listen. No, deciding and changing your mind are totally different. You might need to listen to the market, perhaps reinvent things, changing your mind several times based on the market. But keep that decision to succeed, no matter what. Think clearly and ra-

> WHEN YOU MAKE A DEFINITE DECISION, IT IS AS IF THE UNIVERSE BECOMES AFRAID OF YOU OR STARTS RESPECTING YOU. IT REARRANGES YOUR WAY THE DOORS TO YOUR FORTUNE TO OPEN. AND THE PATH TO YOUR FIRST MILLION SIMPLY BECOMES A MATTER OF TIME.

tionally and follow your decision, your final, disciplined and firm decision to succeed, to become a self-made millionaire. Nothing and no one can stop you on your way to becoming a self-made millionaire.

IT SEEMS LIKE THE UNIVERSE OR THE WORLD SEES THAT SPECIAL DETERMINATION IN YOUR EYES.

There are no weak or strong moments when you decide. It seems like the universe or the world sees that special determination in your eyes. Once we step into the decision frame, where there is no stepping back, once we honestly and passionately with all our heart decide, then there is something truly magical about that decision and mindset that helps create the magic. Remember: Deciding is truly an incredible step in creating your first million. It helps the magic ritual bring its magic. When a mother lifts a car to save her child, it is as if the whole universe is helping her and magic happens. In reality, she cannot do it alone physically alone. She could go to the gym and train there for all her life and it still wouldn't be possible. But in her incredible decision, which is bigger and stronger than herself, something magical happens. The

WHEN A MOTHER LIFTS A CAR TO SAVE HER CHILD, IT IS AS IF THE WHOLE UNIVERSE IS HELPING HER AND MAGIC HAPPENS.

universe gathers itself together and helps her lift the car to save her child. She created magic. It goes beyond her previous beliefs and expectations. And you can do the same in your life with your millions.

There is another part to creating true magic. Once you make a definite decision it also shows you know how to make it all possible. You have figured out how to convert an idea, which is really a bunch of thoughts, into a sustainable business idea. In the end, it will bring your first million, and then after that, many more millions. Converting intangible ideas to tangible products or services is akin to creating magic. It is a process that helps create something that is not tangible into money pouring into your bank account. We call this process materialization. Changing thoughts into reality. Changing thoughts into value for your cus-

> YOUR BUSINESS IS A BUSINESS ONLY IF IT CREATES MASSIVE VALUE FOR YOUR CUSTOMERS.

> MATERIALIZING THOUGHTS IS OFTEN CREATED BY STRONG BELIEFS, SIMPLY BELIEVING IN ONESELF, AND IN THE WHOLE IDEA THAT WE ARE ABOUT TO CREATE.

tomers. Your business is a business only if it creates massive value for your customers.

Materializing thoughts is often created by strong beliefs, simply believing in oneself, and in the whole idea that we are about to create. But most importantly, one must believe his or her idea or goal has great potential, that we are creating something bigger than ourselves, and we must continually keep this vision in mind. Imagine that a powerful belief is like a chair with four legs. If your goal is to sit on that chair, having four strong legs helps you sit down with your whole body weight, feeling confident about it. On the other hand, if the chair has one or two broken legs, then it cannot support you when you want to sit on it. In the same way, a powerful belief about yourself and your capabilities, can help you be more proactive and help you materialize your thoughts. When you believe in yourself, believe in what you do, and you can create magic. Magic can happen. Self-made millionaires all have

powerful beliefs that help them create magic.

BELIEFS, STRONG,
POWERFUL, INSPIRING
BELIEFS, HELP
MATERIALIZE THOUGHTS.

Even when no one else believes
in his or her vision, self-made millionaires persist. Their strong be-
liefs help them move mountains of obstacles that come before of them. Beliefs, strong, powerful, inspiring beliefs, help
materialize thoughts. We can create strong beliefs by observing others that have made it, by reading and studying inspiring people, with strong and powerful affirmations about new
beliefs, and with visualizations about our new behavior.

An important part of creating magic is expanding one's
beliefs. People believe more, when they observe themselves
striving to improve, to become better and better, bringing
more value to customers. We already talked about it in the
first four rituals, but here it is important as a part of changing your belief system. If you are self-employed or you work
for someone else, you must become the best you can be and
believe in yourself. It doesn't matter whether or not you are
a one man band or a business with thousands of people, you
need to create excellence and pro-
vide value. Believe that you can do
it and believe that you can provide
great value for the customer. Value in the eyes of customers helps
in creating magic.

VALUE IN THE EYES OF
CUSTOMERS HELPS IN
CREATING MAGIC.

You can also influence your beliefs and create powerful
beliefs by improving the work that you do. Creating excellence can be done by repetition, by repetition of same process again and again, with passion and patience. Repetition

and excellence strongly influence beliefs. To an external observer, becoming rich might seem boring. The staying in line ritual and the going extra mile ritual are similar at this point in the process and thus expand beliefs. New beliefs create new expectations. New expectations create new behavior. New behavior creates different results. Results lead to your millions. That is one way to create magic. Changing beliefs in

NEW BELIEFS CREATE NEW EXPECTATIONS. NEW EXPECTATIONS CREATE NEW BEHAVIOR. NEW BEHAVIOR CREATES DIFFERENT RESULTS. RESULTS LEAD TO YOUR MILLIONS. THAT IS ONE WAY TO CREATE MAGIC. CHANGING BELIEFS IN THE UNCONSCIOUS MIND.

the unconscious mind. It is like opening eyes. Some people, after focusing on changing beliefs, suddenly create magic. The change happens suddenly, simply as a result of persistence, repetition, new beliefs and expectations. Several of the self-made millionaires made their first million by virtue of an opportunity, an opportunity that took place after months or years or decades of hard work. Working hard not only on the business and creating value, but also on expanding beliefs and boundaries. To an outside observer, many times it looks like luck, but in reality it is far from it. Luck or a chance is only useful when we believe in it, when we expect it, when we see it and when we are ready to exploit it.

Sometimes people say they become rich overnight by luck. They used the first six rituals, but they also became self-made millionaires because they were ready to create the magic. Change using simple belief-changing techniques and be ready for the magic to happen in your life. Self-made millionaires made a definite decision, they materialized their thoughts and they believed in themselves. Those three mental activities then lead to being able to exploit opportunities.

Thinking about how you can materialize your ideas is natural for some ideas that you consider easy. What do you do to connect the dots or what do you do in other areas of your life, where you simply take action and get results? You have already produced results in many areas. What kind of recipe did you use then? It is like a chef thinking about how to combine different foods and in what order, to make a great meal. Your goal would be to look for the magic that would include combining the six rituals with this one and simply make it happen. You know what you want, you will take passionate action, you will go the extra mile, stay in line, and do all necessary things honestly, with great people around you. The only thing now left is to make it happen.

Let me give you my example. The magic ritual was introduced into my life by me, when I simply decided to do it. One Christmas eve my 80-year-old grandmother gave me a gift. I brought her my gift and gave her my best wishes. She did not know what I wanted for Christmas, so she said that she would give me a bit of money and told me that I could go out and buy anything I wanted. I can still remember her hard working hands and her face when she gave me the money, which was not much. But for me, it was an incredible lesson. She had very little money, but she knew how to manage it and was able to give it to me. Many times we forget simple truths. It is not important how much money we make, but also

I MADE MY FIRM AND DEFINITE DECISION: I AM GOING TO MATERIALIZE MY IDEAS; I AM GOING TO MAKE THEM HAPPEN. I WILL CREATE MAGIC. NO WAY BACK.

how much money we spend.

That Christmas eve I was truly touched. I was working on my career, struggling with money and did not know what to do; but I was old enough and capable enough to provide for my family and also to help my grandmother or anyone else that might need it. But instead of me helping her, she helped me.

MATERIALIZE WHAT IS INSIDE OF YOU. SPEND TIME CREATING A GREAT INNER WORLD BECAUSE IT WILL PUSH YOU TO PRODUCE MAGIC IN THE OUTER WORLD.

That moment of truth, along with her care and support, was so emotional that I broke into tears. I wanted to help her but I couldn't, not in the way that I truly wanted. Therefore I decided for good; enough is enough. I will go out and make things happen. I will implement the six rituals and think about how to work on the seventh ritual. I wanted to figure out how to make things really happen. I made my firm and definite decision: I am going to materialize my ideas; I am going to make them happen. I will create magic. No way back. That led me to work on other parts of the magic ritual, expanding boundaries, combining other rituals and combining all the necessary ingredients that make things happen.

When I look back now, it seems so simple. I never could understand the saying that all the abundance, all the money, all the millions that we want are all around us. We are not open, not seeing the boundaries, not open to seeing the magic. And I know now that I was blind, I could not see that opportunities. I did not listen to my inner voice. I was not creating or materializing what was inside of me. Materialize what is inside of you. Spend time creating a great inner world because it will push you to produce magic in the outer world.

Writing this book is one of the ways to materialize or create magic in my life. But a simple decision, a simple moment of inspiration and break-through set my new direction toward wealth and abundance. More money and more abundance in my life. More value and more positive experiences for my customers. I therefore invite you to do the same. Look for inspiration. Start on your inside, and then the inside will push you to create it on the outside. It is truly magical.

THE MAGIC RITUAL IS ABOUT MATERIALIZING THOUGHTS, EXPANDING BOUNDARIES, USING MORE OF YOUR POTENTIAL AND CREATING MASSIVE VALUE FOR THE WORLD AND YOUR CUSTOMERS. GO FOR IT. CREATE MAGIC. CREATE YOUR FIRST MILLION. START NOW OR AFTER YOU FINISH READING THIS BOOK. EITHER WAY IS SOON ENOUGH.

Say to yourself: "Enough is enough. I am going to make something amazing, special and meaningful in my life. My love and passion will be to use the seven rituals and constantly improve what I do so that it will bring great value to my customers and to the world and make myself a self-made millionaire, a rich and happy person." And go out and use your full potential. Consider how you would materialize your goals and wishes. Think how you can make something huge, expand your boundaries, make a firm and definite decision and bring excellence and massive value and tons of positive experiences to your customers. The magic ritual is about materializing thoughts, expanding boundaries, using more of your potential and creating massive value for the world and your customers. Go for it. Create magic. Create your first million. Start now or after you finish reading this book. Either way is soon enough.

Figure 9: CREATE MAGIC RITUAL

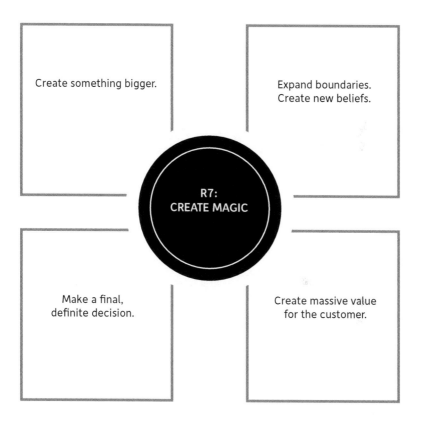

Create something bigger.

Expand boundaries.
Create new beliefs.

R7:
CREATE MAGIC

Make a final,
definite decision.

Create massive value
for the customer.

SELF ASSESSMENT QUESTIONS – YOUR MILLIONAIRE METER FOR RITUAL NUMBER 7 CREATE MAGIC:

- How well do you create and materialize your goals?
- What were some things, which you first thought were hard to achieve, that you eventually successfully completed?
- How can you use the same magic creation for becoming a self-made millionaire?
- How persistent are you in your desires?
- Do you allow yourself to seize opportunities?
- Do you look to creating magic and creating abundance in your life?
- Did you make firm and definite decisions?
- How could you bring more value to your customers?
- How could your materialize or make your ideas turn into reality?

TIPS THAT CAN HELP YOU BECOME A MILLIONAIRE BY BEING CREATING MAGIC:

- Create magic in your life.

- Always work hard to follow your dreams.

- Be creative and keep your eyes open.

- Magic is created by maintaining a clear focus, determination, hard work and persistence. After a while, the doors to your first million can magically open.

- Create your big, bold goals, write down why you would like to achieve them, and how it may change the world for the better.

- Decide. Make a definitive, firm and clear decision.

- Expand your boundaries, grow, and improve.

- Strive for excellence to create more and more value in your customers' lives.

- Ask yourself each morning, "How can I improve the lives of people even more?"

SELF-MADE MILLIONAIRE IMPLEMENTATION LIST TO DO

Which activities can you do in the short run and which in the long run in order to make the magic happen for you? How can you create and materialize the ideas into your life? What can help you create magic? Consider some practical steps for this ritual and how this can become an important part of your life.

SELF-MADE MILLIONAIRE IMPLEMENTATION LIST TO DO

What are you going to do?	By when?	Your accountability partner

Your work is going to fill a large part of your life, and the only way to be truly satisfied is to do what you believe is great work. And the only way to do great work is to love what you do. If you haven't found it yet, keep looking. Don't settle. As with all matters of the heart, you'll know when you find it. And, like any great relationship, it just gets better and better as the years roll on. So keep looking until you find it. Don't settle.

STEVE JOBS

CREATE A PLAN TO BECOME A SELF-MADE MILLIONAIRE

You have now received a map – a map that can help you become a self made millionaire when you introduce the seven rituals into your life. You can adjust them to

IF YOU DO NOTHING AND YOU SIMPLY STAY HOME AND WAIT, I CAN ASSURE YOU THAT YOU WILL NOT BECOME A SELF-MADE MILLIONAIRE.

your personality and to your vision, creating a formula that can help you bring millions and millions into your life. I emphasize the word 'can,' of course, which means that there is absolutely no warranty. I cannot give you one. No one could. But I can assure you that if you do nothing and you simply stay home and wait, I can assure you that you will not become a self-made millionaire unless you fall into a special scenario like inheriting a fortune, winning the lottery, etc. Even if your plan is to win a lottery, you need to take make some sort of plan, when and where to buy the ticket and then action, which means that you might need to buy at least one ticket in order to act upon that plan. Therefore, the lessons in the book are only worthwhile if you decide to implement them. The ideas and rituals that you have studied will be of value if you plan when and how to use them and practice using them. Many times when I talk about these rituals people say to me that they know them, but they do not implement them. Remember, if you know what you need to do, but you do not do it, it means that you just do not know it is enough. Study more. Read more books. Read this book again and again, invite your mastermind members to help you, talk about the rituals with them, introduce the rituals and be persistent and be patient. Some of the exercises might become easier to implement with help from your accountability partner.

THEREFORE, THE LESSONS IN THE BOOK ARE ONLY WORTHWHILE IF YOU DECIDE TO IMPLEMENT THEM. THE IDEAS AND RITUALS THAT YOU HAVE STUDIED WILL BE OF VALUE IF YOU PLAN WHEN AND HOW TO USE THEM AND PRACTICE USING THEM.

ONLY IF YOU TAKE ACTION WILL THE BOOK BRING ANY REAL VALUE TO YOU. IT IS THE REASON THAT I WROTE THIS BOOK.

And if you decide to do nothing, then the actual value of this road map and all the time we spent together, adds up to zero. Only if you take action will the book bring any real value to you. It is the reason that I wrote this book. Remember that you are in control of your life and your everyday rituals. When you were a child your parents or your guardians probably introduced a ritual of brushing your teeth every single day. This ritual has helped you to stay healthy, to be able to talk to strangers in public as well as to have proper oral hygiene. The rituals that you introduce into your life today will have an impact on the results that you receive tomorrow. Focus on building up your rituals today, plan how to integrate them into your life. What you do today will bring your desired results tomorrow. While reading this book, you might read many things that you already know. You might read some things that are new to you. While reading the book you might have thought about some new ideas. But I urge you to start creating magic, to start walking and never stop, all the way until your first million, and to your other millions that will follow. The value of the book is worthless if you stop after a few steps. And tomorrow it might be too late.

So why wait? Why not introducing the steps into your life today? Implement the seven rituals into your life and allow them to become as natural as all of your other rituals brushing your teeth. Make the seven rituals of self made millionaires compulsory. Below you will find a few tips. Take full responsibility for your life. Not your parents, not your environment, not the economy, not your past decisions, not any of your current life circumstances, absolutely nothing can be the cause of you not taking complete action right now, at this very moment. Go out, with all your heart, with all your passion and give your best to this planet. I believe that this is your path to becoming a self-made millionaire. Your path is unique to you. Use the

> FOCUS ON BUILDING UP YOUR RITUALS TODAY, PLAN HOW TO INTEGRATE THEM INTO YOUR LIFE. WHAT YOU DO TODAY WILL BRING YOUR DESIRED RESULTS TOMORROW.

> TAKE FULL RESPONSIBILITY FOR YOUR LIFE. NOT YOUR PARENTS, NOT YOUR ENVIRONMENT, NOT THE ECONOMY, NOT YOUR PAST DECISIONS, NOT ANY OF YOUR CURRENT LIFE CIRCUMSTANCES, ABSOLUTELY NOTHING CAN BE THE CAUSE OF YOU NOT TAKING COMPLETE ACTION RIGHT NOW, AT THIS VERY MOMENT.

seven rituals as much as you can in a way that will serve you best. Develop your own rituals, which will bring you to your first million. Every time you blame the outside world for whatever you are facing in your life, you are moving away from your goals and away from becoming a self-made millionaire. Excuses are a complete waste of time. Taking full responsibility for your life is not so easy. Sometimes it even hurts, but if that is what you need to do to succeed and be free.

I discourage crazy excuses. Some people say they are too young, too old, too tall, too short, that they do not have the money, do not have the education, the economy is not right and the circumstances are wrong or that the people are not ready for their products and services. Stop, stop, stop. It is time to make a different plan. There are people in the world that have been young, old, without education in the worst economic times, beaten, sick, broken, bankrupt or who faced several life challenges and they found the energy, they found the inner strength to pursue their dreams and they made things happen. One of my heroes is Nick Vujicic, a great speaker, who was born without arms and legs. He travels around the world and has inspired literally millions and millions of people. Look for role models of self-made millionaires who have succeeded. They are the ones who have managed to become self-made millionaires in times when everyone else was losing money. There are people that simply went out and followed their heart, passion, and dreams and became self-made millionaires. And now it is your time, time to stop making excuses.

Taking full responsibility, and letting go of any excuses, can bring you more choices as well as more motivation as you move towards your goals. Think of other things that you do in life that you simply go out and do, without excuses. Do the same with your first million. And have fun with your excuses, smile at what you think, be full of curiosity with all of your crazy beliefs and excuses. The more you have fun, the more you laugh. You will find more joy and more freedom. Fun expands creativity and brings more results and more dedication into your life.

So, make sure you have fun while you do it. Life is too short to not fully enjoy it. Live life fully and the more you love what you do, the more your customers and your colleagues will notice, and all that love will bring you great results. Loving what you do and having fun will help you in moments when there might be rain in your life. Remember that if there is rain, there is a sun just waiting behind the clouds. And after a rain, the sky is blue and clear, truly and honestly full of that wonderful energy for a new beginning, a new day.

Have faith and persist. I believe in you. I believe that inside of you there is a greatness, which if you show half of it to this world, it would pleasantly surprise you, as well as the world around you. You have loads of potential for cre-

> TAKING FULL RESPONSIBILITY, AND LETTING GO OF ANY EXCUSES, CAN BRING YOU MORE CHOICES AS WELL AS MORE MOTIVATION AS YOU MOVE TOWARDS YOUR GOALS.

> HAVE FAITH AND PERSIST. I BELIEVE IN YOU. I BELIEVE THAT INSIDE OF YOU THERE IS A GREATNESS, WHICH IF YOU SHOW HALF OF IT TO THIS WORLD, IT WOULD PLEASANTLY SURPRISE YOU, AS WELL AS THE WORLD AROUND YOU. YOU HAVE LOADS OF POTENTIAL FOR CREATING MILLIONS. UNLOCK IT.

ating millions. Unlock it. Persist in improving and persist in your special calling. Every person on this planet has a calling that is unique for that person. Use that calling to create your first million and all the following millions. Make sure that you have fun while you use your calling to create wealth and abundance.

Compare your life and your results with no one. There is no need for competition. The seven rituals are only here to help you lead the way, the way you choose. Use them as much as you can and use them to support your life's mission in the best way that you can. You are unique and your life is unique. No matter how young or how old, no matter how much formal education you have, become a lifelong learner, and remember that there are many, many opportunities for you.

Set a goal by which you will help other people to become millionaires once you get there. Make a plan for implementing that goal. My goal is to speak (face to face or through video or any other communication channel such as this book) to over 1.111.111.111 people around the world by October 13, 2081, when I will be 107 years old. My goal is to also create 10,000 new self-made millionaires by December 31, 2024. Please help me by becoming one. Now you know my birthday if you want to send me a birthday card. If you wish, please do so. I would be happy to hear how well

> **SET A GOAL BY WHICH YOU WILL HELP OTHER PEOPLE TO BECOME MILLIONAIRES ONCE YOU GET THERE. MAKE A PLAN FOR IMPLEMENTING THAT GOAL.**

> **MY GOAL IS TO ALSO CREATE 10,000 NEW SELF-MADE MILLIONAIRES BY DECEMBER 31, 2024. PLEASE HELP ME BY BECOMING ONE.**

you are doing and how close you are to your first, second, tenth million. Anyhow, I believe that as I go forth and help others achieve their goals, it comes back to me. So help others by sharing your tips with them, your unique way of implementing the seven rituals. And once you create the magic, start all over again, in a new direction with new goals.

CREATE YOUR OWN UNIQUE PLAN TO BECOME A SELF-MADE MILLIONAIRE AND CREATE YOUR OWN UNIQUE PATH THAT WILL ENABLE YOU TO LIVE YOUR DREAMS AND TO LIVE TO YOUR FULL POTENTIAL.

Create your own unique plan to become a self-made millionaire and create your own unique path that will enable you to live your dreams and to live to your full potential. Other people's examples and other people as your heroes can help you develop great rituals, great values and great strategies and beliefs. But your path is unique, and it should be like that. Creating your unique way based on the basic principles and rituals is something that I strongly recommend. Live your dreams. Express your potential. Be who you really are. Do not pretend to be someone else. Be yourself.

Figure 10: NEVERENDING CYCLE OF IMPLEMENTING THE 7 RITUALS

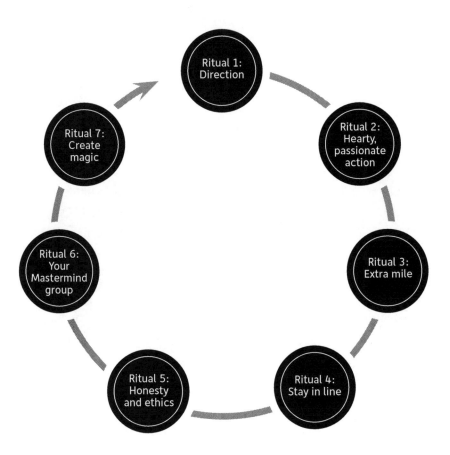

Just play.
Have fun.
Enjoy the game.

MICHAEL JORDAN

HAVE FUN

In the next chapter I am going to ask you write your millionaire statement, a statement that can help you become a self-made millionaire. Before doing that, let me briefly describe to you an important lesson that I did not want you to miss. We never met face to face, so I know little about you, and I am also not sure how old you are and how many more years you plan to live. The number is not actually important at all. You might live one more year and you might have many decades in front of you and I certainly wish the latter for you. A year or a decade seems rather long when you think of it, but in reality it flies by quickly and sometimes it seems like a short moment when you look at it. Life is too short to make it too serious or boring. Enjoy life. Enjoy your way to becoming a self-made millionaire.

A YEAR OR A DECADE SEEMS RATHER LONG WHEN YOU THINK OF IT, BUT IN REALITY IT FLIES BY QUICKLY AND SOMETIMES IT SEEMS LIKE A SHORT MOMENT WHEN YOU LOOK AT IT. LIFE IS TOO SHORT TO MAKE IT TOO SERIOUS OR BORING. ENJOY LIFE. ENJOY YOUR WAY TO BECOMING A SELF-MADE MILLIONAIRE.

I have studied for many years, running my businesses while spending time training people. During these years, I learned how important it is to have fun and enjoy life. How wonderful it is to feel inner peace and joy with what I do. And I want it to be fun for you as well. Make sure to include in your millionaire statement your commitment to having fun. Picking up a topic or an area of work that you love will certainly help you because when you are working, it will actually not feel like you are working at all.

When you love what you do and you do what you love, life and work are so much easier and special. When rainy days come, it feels so much easier to wait for the sunshine, but at the same time, when you love what you do, even a rainy day is ten times better than a normal day at a boring job, which you hate. So think of something that you really love doing and look at how you can fall in love again with what you do. What is great about what you do? Think of people who you really love to spend time with and work with. Select what you want and who you will do it with, who will be the people around you, helping you achieve what you want to achieve.

Look to have fun. So many people have instilled unhappy, unconscious formulas in themselves. For example: I will be happy when I get to the million or when I achieve what I want to achieve. This is a formula that means one cannot be happy without that achievement. Look at your own formulas. Did you decide what will bring you happi-

> WHEN YOU LOVE WHAT YOU DO AND YOU DO WHAT YOU LOVE, LIFE AND WORK ARE SO MUCH EASIER AND SPECIAL.

> SO MANY PEOPLE HAVE INSTILLED UNHAPPY, UNCONSCIOUS FORMULAS IN THEMSELVES. FOR EXAMPLE: I WILL BE HAPPY WHEN I GET TO THE MILLION OR WHEN I ACHIEVE WHAT I WANT TO ACHIEVE. THIS IS A FORMULA THAT MEANS ONE CANNOT BE HAPPY WITHOUT THAT ACHIEVEMENT.

ness in your life? Make your happiness formula simpler, so you will be happy and have fun all the way to your millions. When I first looked at my formula and understood it, it felt so stupid, especially because none of that was true, it was only in my imagination. And when I observed many of the self-made millionaires, many of them were thrilled with learning something new. New technologies, new ways to do business, all that could help them improve their business or some sort of process in their jobs. Find small and simple ways to be happy along the way.

TAKE A DEEP BREATH AND ACKNOWLEDGE WITH GRATITUDE WHAT YOU HAVE ACHIEVED.

MAKE EVERY STEP TO YOUR MILLIONS FUN.

It is normal that people, once they reach their first milestone, continue to generate new goals. So after they reach a first or a second million, they go for a third one and continue raising the bar. While doing that, stop for a moment, take a deep breath and acknowledge with gratitude what you have achieved. You can celebrate and have fun on the way to your goals, do not wait until the end. Therefore, I would like to invite you to commit to having fun, to doing what you love to do and doing it more often, and then enjoy doing it.

One of the ways to do this is to exaggerate every step. Think of it as important and magical and truly a blessing. Make every step to your millions fun. When you look from the perspective of someone who does not have your opportunities, who does not live the life of his or her dreams, then, at the end of the day, you can say that you are privileged to be someone special. You are someone who is able to fight for your dreams. Richard Branson's general attitude to life is to enjoy every minute of every day. He never does anything with a feeling of, "Oh God, I've got to do this today." Look to how you can have a similar approach to your every day routines and the new rituals that you are going to introduce.

HAVE FUN. I WOULD LIKE TO INVITE YOU TO JOIN ME, AND LET'S BECOME SELF-MADE MILLIONAIRES THAT SIMPLY HAVE FUN AND ENJOY LIFE.

Have fun. I would like to invite you to join me, and let's become self-made millionaires that simply have fun and enjoy life. Let us be part of the group of people who have fun, so that you become a self-made millionaire that will have fun with every single step that you take on your way to becoming one. But remember the right order. First introduce the rituals, have fun, be happy and become a self-made millionaire; and remain happy and still have fun. Please do not wait to be happy and have fun after the rituals are fully introduced, or worse, until you make your millions. Many times the habit of being too serious, or not having fun, will stay with you. You can and will create inspiration for many people who would like to follow what you do. Become an important member of the group of self-made millionaires that will have fun, from the first step all the way to the millions.

Freedom is everything and love is all the rest.

DR. RICHARD BANDLER

YOUR MILLIONAIRE STATEMENT

Many times simply writing down your millionaire statement or a goal can help program your unconscious mind. It can also help clearly define what the conscious mind wants from the unconscious.

WRITING DOWN YOUR MILLIONAIRE STATEMENT OR GOAL WILL ALSO HELP YOU MAKE YOUR IDEA OR GOAL CLEARER.

Writing down your millionaire statement or goal will also help you make your idea or goal clearer. Besides writing your goals down, it is also helpful to write down a specific plan to implement your goal. After you have your millionaire statement, do not stop here. Also prepare a plan for how you are going to get there. How are you going to achieve what you are going to achieve? While you are writing it, make sure you are filled with energy and motivated to achieve what you want to achieve. Find photos from magazines that are part of your dreams and plans, so that you can visualize your achievement along with your goals. It is important that you first think of what you are going to create using sensory words to describe your goal in pictures, sounds, feelings and perhaps even in smells and tastes. What is the smell of your success? What is the taste of becoming a self-made millionaire? Be specific and also be vivid, as much as possible, but also think about bigger things. How is this going to impact the world around you? What will you bring to the world, to the people around you and for yourself? So writing down the 'what' is part of the first ritual – the direction ritual, but it has a great influence on all the other rituals, as well. If you want to have your millionaire year this year, put small posted notes or stickers all over your house, in your bathroom, kitchen, living room, bedroom. Some people that have used this technique have even put posted notes with their millionaire goal in the fridge.

BE SPECIFIC AND ALSO BE VIVID, AS MUCH AS POSSIBLE, BUT ALSO THINK ABOUT BIGGER THINGS. HOW IS THIS GOING TO IMPACT THE WORLD AROUND YOU?

IMAGINE YOURSELF ALSO BEING CERTAIN ABOUT YOUR SUCCESS, FEEL HOW YOU WOULD FEEL WITH ALL THAT CERTAINTY. WRITE DOWN WITH THAT SAME CERTAINTY AND DETERMINATION, HOW YOU ARE GOING TO INTEGRATE YOUR GOALS INTO YOUR LIFE.

Write down your definite decision to become a self-made millionaire, describe in great detail how you are going to introduce the seven rituals into your everyday life. Warren Buffet said he always knew he was going to be rich, he never doubted it for a minute. Imagine yourself also being certain about your success, feel how you would feel with all that certainty. Write down with that same certainty and determination, how you are going to integrate your goals into your life. The door of the self-made millionaires club is open to you, me and to everyone on this planet.

Remember to sign and date the millionaire statement and

write it with energy. Read it with great energy. Personally, I like to be standing, even jumping with some great inspirational and action music. Remember that if a sales person wants to make a sale, he or she must first sell the product or service to him- or herself. If you want your unconscious mind to buy what you are consciously selling, you need to make it as believable as possible. Your body, your voice and tone, every cell of your body must believe in it. If you do affirmations, do them with power and energy. Your millionaire statement might be changing all the time, but your energy, your determination, your beliefs should remain as high as possible. So stand up, say who you would like to become, how you would like to behave and fill your body with great energy resulting from your affirmations as you read your millionaire statement again and again. Read your millionaire statement with great energy at least ten times every morning when you wake up and ten times in the evening when you go to sleep. You are more suggestible when you wake up and just before you go to sleep. And while you sleep and dream, your uncon-

REMEMBER TO SIGN AND DATE THE MILLIONAIRE STATEMENT AND WRITE IT WITH ENERGY. READ IT WITH GREAT ENERGY.

IF YOU WANT YOUR UNCONSCIOUS MIND TO BUY WHAT YOU ARE CONSCIOUSLY SELLING, YOU NEED TO MAKE IT AS BELIEVABLE AS POSSIBLE.

READ YOUR MILLIONAIRE STATEMENT WITH GREAT ENERGY AT LEAST TEN TIMES EVERY MORNING WHEN YOU WAKE UP AND TEN TIMES IN THE EVENING WHEN YOU GO TO SLEEP. YOU ARE MORE SUGGESTIBLE WHEN YOU WAKE UP AND JUST BEFORE YOU GO TO SLEEP.

scious mind might start making unconscious changes. When you are driving, you can state your millionaire statement again and again to program your unconscious mind. And it makes you feel good.

What you may want to include in your millionaire statement is why you want to become a self-made millionaire, and who are the people who look up to you and you might inspire by becoming a self-made millionaire. Also you may want to include why you want to become a self-made millionaire in terms of what you are going to be able to afford for your loved ones, and what you are going to be able to afford for yourself. Some people like to include in the statement which great charities or people they are going to help. You also may want to include all the toys or all things that might become a part of your new life. A strong and inspiring 'why' will increase your passion and determination. A strong and inspiring 'why' will help you stay focused, inspired and motivated during days when you might want to go out of your line. A strong and inspiring 'why' will help you go the extra mile. A strong and inspiring 'why' will help you work with integrity and honesty. A strong and inspiring 'why' will attract people who can help you achieve what you want to achieve. When you know why you are doing what you are doing, magic happens.

A journey of a thousand miles begins with a single step.

LAO-TZU

Step 1:

What do you want? Remember, the clearer you define this, the better. Remember to write down what you would like to create. (Don't write down that you want to be a self-made millionaire, but what you want to create. Your millions should be the consequence of the great value you provide to your customers. The abundance is what you get in return for your products or services.)

_____

_____

_____

_____

_____

_____

_____

_____

_____

_____

_____

_____

_____

_____

_____

_____

Step 2:

Why do you want it? Write down a strong and inspiring 'why.' Why would you like to create what you want to create? The first part of your 'why' should be focus on why you create products and services. What do you believe in? What do you stand for? What message would you like your customers to perceive? You can also add why you would like to get the amazing reward of becoming a self-made millionaire, but first do a strong 'why' for products and services that bring value to your customers and change the world for the better. And finally: Who can you help and who could you inspire by becoming a self-made millionaire?

_____

_____

_____

_____

_____

_____

_____

_____

_____

_____

_____

_____

Step 3:

What is your plan? Create a plan. Planning and executing your plan leads you to results. Write down step 1, step 2, step 3, etc. Remember that this is the first draft of your plan, and that it can change. You might even change the very basic idea, what you plan to create. The plan changes or updates should be based on the feedback you receive from other people, from the market, and from your mastermind group. Remember to have a rational, scientific method for evaluation. In the business world you need to have some basic financial literacy and to monitor what you are doing all the time. Keep on improving, refining your plan all the time. Become obsessed in a good way with your constant plan improvement. A plan can be so simple that it will fit below in the space available. But, most likely, it might need to be more detailed, so please take more paper or put it in your computer. Every day take a few small steps towards your goal. Every day!

Step 4:

Create a second plan. This plan is to introduce the seven rituals into your life. It will be the plan for your personal mastery and excellence. Think of becoming the person you would like to become. Remember that your cells change and are replaced every day, so you can become a new and different person with different rituals and different thinking processes in a few years. Think of ways that you can introduce the seven rituals into your life and how will it make a difference. Do not introduce the rituals for the sake of introducing the rituals, but introduce them while you pursue your original plan.

_____

_____

_____

_____

_____

_____

_____

_____

_____

_____

_____

Step 5:

Execute all of your plans and move towards the implementation of your plans every single day. How do you eat an elephant? One bite at a time. Remember to have fun while you do it. Write down ideas about how you can execute your plans with discipline, passion and determination and still have fun, enjoying what you do.

_____

_____

_____

_____

_____

_____

_____

_____

_____

_____

_____

_____

_____

_____

_____

_____

And finally the important YES question from Joseph Campbell: "The big question is whether or not you are going to say a hearty YES to your adventure." And my question is: "Are you going to decide with all your heart to introduce the seven rituals, to have fun all the way and to never, never give up? Are you going to say a hearty YES to your new adventure NOW?"

It has been an honor and a blessing to be able to share the seven rituals with you. I wish you inner peace, happiness, love, joy, and abundance and I pray that soon I will be able to welcome you to the self-made millionaires club. It would be an honor and you will become my inspiration and the inspiration to many more people that will follow. Remember to have fun all the way.

With Love and Support, to your millions,
Dr. Aleksander Šinigoj

P.S.: I have read the book several times and each and every time I found something minor to improve, something to add or change. Please feel free to write me with any improvements, questions, comments or your achievements: as@aleksander-sinigoj.com. As I receive lots of emails every day, please be patient and understanding. Although I try to respond as much as possible I am unable to reply to all emails.

2 FREE TICKETS TO MY '7 RITUALS OF SELF-MADE MILLIONAIRES' WORKSHOP – LIVE

The content of this book is based on the workshop with the same title: 7 RITUALS OF SELF-MADE MILLIONAIRES. If you liked the book and you would like to meet me live, I invite you to join me for the workshop. By having a printed or electronic (Kindle) version of this book, you are entitled to two free tickets for the workshop. Please check if the tickets are valid as it depends on my host and organizer in a particular country or venue. Places are also subject to availability, so book early in advance to reserve your free seat. Not all events and all hosts will accept those tickets, so please be patient for the right date and venue when your tickets will be valid.

If you would like these rituals to be presented to your team and to your staff, please contact me at:
as@aleksandersinigoj.com
to discuss speaking opportunities. As I receive lots of emails every day, please be patient as I am unable to reply all of them.

A FREE AUDIO CD –
MY GIFT TO YOU

After you have purchased and read this book you can download your free mind programming recording, which can help you implement the seven rituals into your life and become a self-made millionaire.

You can download the link from:

www.aleksandersinigoj.com/7rituals

The value of the recording is $97.00 USD. When you use the special promotional code, 7RIT4U, the amount will change to $0 USD and you will be able to download it free of charge. You will receive a link to your email account. Please verify your spam or junk mailbox, in case the link goes there directly.

We recommend you use a headset or earphones for better effect and that you do not listen to the recording while driving or operating any machinery, which requires your full attention. Only listen to it when you can relax completely.

The ones who are crazy enough to think that they can change the world are the ones who do.

STEVE JOBS

Dr. Aleksander Šinigoj is an inspirational and motivational writer and speaker. His focus is on how to improve and change people's thinking and unconscious programming. His books have one common goal: touching and changing lives around the world. To absorb his books into the unconscious mind, he recommends reading his books more than once. To produce results in life he is a true believer of taking action. But taking action from feeling inspired and determined, rather than taking action out of fear, greed or any other negative emotion. His books are about change, but not only change on the conscious, but also on the unconscious level.

Through four-dimensional mind programming approaches, Aleksander has helped, and continues to help, people around the world to become better and to change their thoughts, feelings and, in the end, their behavior. When people behave differently they get different results. He is now traveling the world and speaking to different organizations that would like to produce different results by changing the values, beliefs, strategies and behaviors of their people. His fun, passionate, warm and mesmerizing way of presenting different topics makes his speeches and trainings special, addictive and unique.

Made in the USA
Charleston, SC
24 September 2016